Hide and Seek

How I lost and found my baby through adoption

LIFESUCCESS PUBLISHING, LLC
8900 E Pinnacle Peak Road, Suite D240
Scottsdale, AZ 85255

Telephone: 800.473.7134
Fax: 480.661.1014
E-mail: admin@lifesuccesspublishing.com

ISBN (hardcover): 978-1-59930-204-1
ISBN (e-book): 978-1-59930-285-0

Cover : Daniela A. Savone, LifeSuccess Publishing, LLC
Text: Daniela A. Savone, LifeSuccess Publishing, LLC

Printed in Canada

Hide and Seek

How I lost and found my baby through adoption

Janet Stuessi

Dedication

This book is dedicated to the memory of my mother, Jacqueline, and her beloved friend Marjorie.

I believe they have inspired me to be a devoted mother and friend.

Contents

Foreword

I wrote this book twenty years ago, the year I found my son. It has been sitting in a drawer in a Pee-Chee (a folder) hidden away for all these years. My daughter and I went to a book writing conference and for the heck of it, I took the book with me. When I left the seminar, I decided to have it published.

My intent is to not hurt anyone by telling my story; therefore, some of the names have been changed. I hope this book will help people to understand the adoption triad, (birthparents, adoptees, and adoptive parents). The choices we make can alter lives, and if there is something we need to make right, there is courage within us to accomplish that goal.

Part 1 of the book is my story, and Part 2 is a guide to pregnancy and the choices birthmothers and birthfathers face. If a woman chooses the adoption route, the guide will help her make an informed decision by explaining the choices that can affect all involved. If you have already surrendered a child to adoption, the guide can help you decide if a search is right for you. And if so, it will aid you in how to prepare for your search and, hopefully, an eventual reunion.

I recently saw the movie *The Duchess* set in 1700s England, where the Duchess has to make the decision to give up her baby daughter. The heart-wrenching scene in which she hands over her baby has been played out through the ages and still rings true today. My belief is that every mother should be given the opportunity to keep her child. If it is not possible, the best option, in my view, is an open or semi-open adoption arrangement. Years ago, before all the laws and social mores were set, a child could know his/her birthmother, but be parented by someone else. Secrets serve no purpose and always cause grief. Yet, over time, they are almost always exposed. Why not be forthcoming at the start of the child's life?

Some time ago, society made the decision that these children needed to be hidden away, which caused shame not only upon the birthmother, but in many instances, to the child. The only shame should be upon those who forcefully dictate what a pregnant woman should do, giving no thought to the consequences. Shame on those who put in place these mores and social standards.

My son calls me "Jan." Neither he nor I refer to me as his "mother," nor would I want to be. That title should only be given to the woman who raised him. Even though I don't feel I have the right to be called his mother, in my heart he will always be my son.

Acknowledgments

The most important things in my life are my family and friends. I am happiest when I am in their company. My accomplishments are the relationships I have with them; thank you one and all. Thanks to my husband, Roger; to my two daughters, Julie and Karen; to my son, who graciously let us into his life; to Mom and Dad, who supported me through my life; and to my five sisters. I thank and adore you. There are many people not mentioned in the book who have taken me into their hearts and have supported me. I thank you, too.

Thank you to my sister Barb and my friends of more than forty-five years—Veronica, Sandy, and Mary. There isn't a step I could have taken without your support and love.

A special thanks to Jana who helped me with all aspects of the book; especially the second part, the guide to pregnancy. And to my sister Pam who edited *Hide and Seek* with me well into the night—thank you for your hard work.

I have to thank People Synergistically Involved (PSI) Seminars—a personal growth and development company. This group has had a tremendous influence on my life and on the lives of my husband and children. The seminars have helped me to believe anything is possible. It was at one of the seminars that I made the decision to pursue the possibility of finding my son.

I also want to give a special acknowledgment to adoptive parents who have unselfishly opened their hearts and their homes. Thank you for your commitment and devotion to our children. To Dave's parents, I will always be grateful.

And finally, thank you to Gerry Robert and Bob Proctor, who inspired me to take the steps to have this book published.

PART ONE:
Janet's Journey

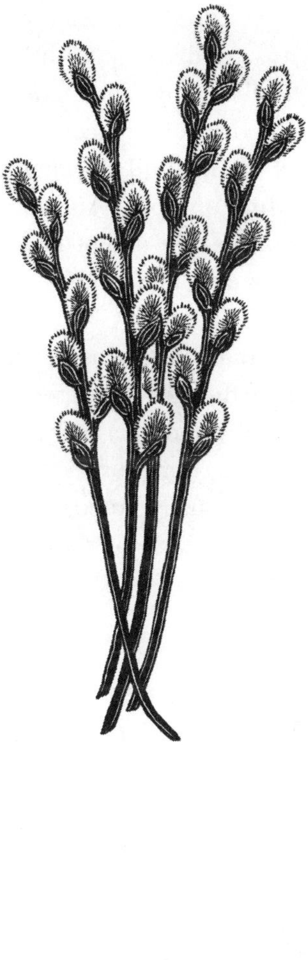

I was born on February 28, 1949—the first of six girls. My mother, Jackie, was a native of Seattle, and my father, John, hailed from Idaho. They were our personal John and Jackie, just like the Kennedys. My mother was the youngest of three girls, and Dad was an only child.

I lived a fortunate life because both sets of grandparents lived within miles of our home. We visited regularly, and there was always someone to do activities with and shower us with love. We could tromp off by ourselves whenever we wanted and walk to any one of their homes. Erna, my mom's mother, often invited my sister Barb and me for sleepovers. For us, it was a huge treat that she gave us the big TV dinners that came with dessert in the tray. We would play the card game Canasta for hours with her. My dad's mother, Verle, let us play dress up with her costume jewelry and high heels. We sat in her kitchen while she made homemade noodles and baked pies. Those were the days of innocence when you could venture anywhere by yourself, meet friends, and play on the school playground for hours. You simply said, "Mom, I'm off." And she would reply, "Be home by 5:30 for dinner," and that was the end of it. Dinner was always served promptly at 5:30 PM, and you didn't dare miss it.

We have countless photos of Barb and me as very little girls in dresses made by our grandmother, with white gloves, petticoats, little patent leather Mary Jane shoes, and hats worn atop perfectly curled hair. In those days, for holidays and special events, our mother dressed us immaculately—always in our finest. We were usually posed in one of our grandparents' yards in front of a beautiful rose bush or rhododendron. We typified the Norman Rockwell paintings of the time.

Airplanes played an important role in our lives because my dad was an airline pilot. Like so many men of his generation, he learned to fly while he was in the service. Flying was an integral part of spending time with our dad. For example, if the youngest daughter had not flown on a plane trip with Dad by the time she turned five years old, that was considered a sin. Soon they would jet off to experience air travel and the perks of being the daughter of an airline pilot. While it may seem unbelievable, it was common for us to sit in the cockpit with Dad and watch him fly the commercial airliner.

My dad was the neighborhood father who played ball with the kids. When anything broke, the neighborhood kids came to him to fix it—he could fix anything. We were so proud he was our dad and loved hanging out with him. My sisters and I spent countless hours with him in his shop. Most fathers were at work every day; mine was gone for several days at a time, but then he would be home for several. We always anticipated the time we could spend with him.

My mom was raised Catholic and lived a life dedicated to her religion. She tried so hard to do the right thing according to her beliefs, but sometimes things just didn't work. One time she thought it would be a good idea to have her daughters say the rosary before dinner while kneeling around her bed. It was a sweet idea, but it didn't last too long. Someone would inevitably start acting up, trying to make someone else laugh, or we would all start talking too much. Mom would make the guilty party face the wall, but we still found a way to make this experience fun. I don't think it was very fun or spiritual for Mom, so she eventually gave up on the nightly ritual.

Mom sang with the most beautiful voice. As a child, she suffered from terrible asthma, and her doctors prescribed singing lessons to help her breathing. She sang for the troops during WWII and gained some local attention In fact, Bing Crosby invited her to his radio show, but Mom was more interested in seeking the traditional life of marriage and family. As a child, I remember thinking I had the most beautiful mother and handsome father in the whole world. I always marveled at how my mother managed six children. She said it wasn't difficult because our ages were so far apart. (There is a seventeen-year difference between my youngest sister and me.)

My sister Barb is two years younger than I. Growing up, we were inseparable. We learned to rely on each other quite a bit because Mom struggled with her asthma. Many times Mom barely had the strength to just sit in her chair. As the two oldest children, Barb and I learned to help out with our younger sisters. Barb loved the babies, and I loved to cook; so early on we established our roles.

We all attended a Catholic grade school just up the street from our house. It was a very safe neighborhood where you knew all the people and where you were safe just walking to school or playing carefree. During the summer, we often stayed at our beach home on Whidbey Island in Puget Sound. It was a funny little cabin that looked as if someone just kept adding on rooms as they were needed—with the last one being a toilet. Those summer days were glorious. I loved the beach life and still do. It made for a wonderful childhood. I thank God every day for the opportunities I experienced as a child with such a loving family.

My sisters and I were so fortunate to have an amazing father. He made many sacrifices to support his family. But more importantly, he always parented with a calm and loving demeanor. Sometimes my mom would need to attend evening meetings, and Dad would be left to parent. We loved those times. We would prop up the coffee table with some books and magazines and then have races with any little toy with wheels. We always felt sort of rebellious because he would let us stay up past our bedtimes to play with him. Sometimes my mom would catch us; and while I think she secretly found it heartwarming, she always pretended to be unhappy with our staying up too late. Our picture boxes are full of photos with my dad lying on the living room floor playing with us. We might be playing with his hair, or there might be a doll walking up his back. The joy and smiles and love show through every photograph.

My dad was in the military reserves, and the base was just down the hill from our home. There were times we would go watch him take off in his big plane; at times when we heard a plane fly overhead, we knew it was him. All my sisters and I were so proud of him. We felt special to be the daughters of an airline pilot.

His job was demanding and stressful at times. Every six months the pilots had their flight checkups. He carried a big black case that had all the specifications of the planes, new information, and anything else they might test him on. My mom ran interference for him, and if she warned us he was studying for his flight check, then we knew to be really quiet and good.

Mom and Dad also had a rental house to upkeep. Not only did my father worry about his job and supporting his family, he spent extra time keeping up the rental house. I often reflect on the time we spent with him painting, cleaning, and working in the yard at the rental house. He miraculously found time to do so much and still make each of his daughters feel special. I never heard my mom and dad fight. My mom was the disciplinarian in the family because Dad would be gone for lengths of time. You would never hear the words, "Wait until your father gets home," because that might be four days away. Mom simply handled problems as they occurred.

Barb and I spent endless hours playing with dolls, creating song and dance routines, and playing school. Dad jokingly referred to us as the Lemon Sisters. We had a clubhouse in the woods at the end of our street where our meetings were held. Sometimes we set up a little altar in our bedroom and acted out Catholic Mass, smashing white bread into little discs for communion. One of our favorite activities was to travel to the cabin with our grandparents and go fishing. Gramps did everything for us—from baiting the hook to removing the gunk off the hooks that we dragged from the bottom of the sea. I can still hear him singing to the fish, "She wore 'em, she tore 'em, she wore 'em in the winter, she wore 'em in the fall. And when it came to summer, she didn't wear 'em at all!" We adored him.

School proved to be difficult for me, and I suspect I had some kind of learning disability. In those days, there was no testing; so I made it through simply because I was a well-behaved and quiet child and because my teachers liked me. Back then, the social norms and my strict upbringing told me to keep quiet about my difficulties. Children were supposed to be seen and not heard, and we were taught to suffer in silence. Complaining was not an option. I was scared to death of speaking up or asking questions. To me, raising my hand to tell a teacher I didn't understand would have been a fate worse than death.

In my later years of grade school, the world political situation became very scary, especially to children who didn't have a clear concept of world affairs. One of our teachers explained that she was going to relay a story that would seem very horrible. She said that anyone who wanted to leave the room was free to go. I was really shy and didn't want to single myself out, so I stayed to listen. There were so many stories about the Communists. We were frightened by them, although as children I don't think we really had a sense of who "them" actually represented. My teacher told a story of a priest in the Soviet Union who was teaching "The Lord's Prayer" to his class. Communist soldiers rushed into the room and demanded that he stop. When he chose to continue, the soldiers cut out his tongue and then proceeded to pierce the eardrums of all the students. After that story, I had recurring nightmares of Communist soldiers riding horses down the street to our home. They were coming to get us, I was certain!

It's ironic that I had such horrible visions because my childhood is full of wonderful memories, and we felt safe in our neighborhood. But I do remember feeling fearful from all the talk about Communism. I was in the eighth grade when the Bay of Pigs happened, and although I really didn't comprehend the political matters, I just knew it was a very serious and scary time.

Another important part of our lives was our relationship to a family that lived directly across from our backyard fence. Because our backyards met, we could look from one kitchen into the other. My mother and Marge instantly became best friends. In a short time, we built a gate in the fence to allow easy access. Our friends had two children, Mary and Bill.

Mary was two years older than Bill and I. She became my big sister. Bill became the brother we never had, and we fought like it, too. Our families basically blended into one. Our fathers even enjoyed puttering away in each other's workshops. Our neighbors became like our extended family, and we all just felt so blessed to live near each other.

Before my eighth-grade year, we had to decide which high school I would attend. It was a huge decision. My mother graduated from an all-girl school, Holy Angels. My other option was a much larger co-ed Catholic high school that separated students by academic ability. I was fearful of being placed in a "stupid kid" class, so I chose Holy Angels. I met four of my lifelong friends that year. After forty-four years, we are just as close as ever.

I started my freshman year in 1963. I loved my new friends and life at Holy Angels. There were only 250 students and about 50 in my class. Most of the nuns had taught my mom when she attended the school. They all remembered her and her beautiful voice from years ago. I quickly became known as Jackie's daughter. They loved her, and that was fine with me.

The high school was on the top floor directly above a grade school. There was absolutely no talking between classes. We wore the typical private school uniforms consisting of navy blue pleated skirts, sweaters with white blouses, white socks, and Oxford shoes. It was always interesting to see every year what the style in socks would be. Would they be rolled down, pulled all the way up, or knee high? The nuns would have us kneel on the floor to make sure our skirts reached the floor. As soon as we left school for the day, those skirts got rolled up by the waist band until they were as high as we thought would be cool. One time, my sister Barb wore a scarf in her hair. The principal tore it out of her hair, asking if she was "trying to be smart." You didn't dare to be an individual.

Even in the strict environment, we did the silliest things. One time, my classmates and I were sitting in a circle with my friend Veronica seated across from me. I pulled up some skin on my knee and attached a safety pin to it. I whispered for the girls to tell Veronica to look over at me. They passed the message around the circle until it finally reached Veronica. When she looked over and saw the safety pin stuck to my knee, she screamed and got kicked out of class. We did some outlandish things to make the strict atmosphere bearable and more fun.

By the time I started high school, the political situation in our country was really tense. There were many unnerving incidents throughout the nation. The most dramatic and shocking event was President Kennedy's assassination. Shortly thereafter, the news had considerable coverage about a place called Vietnam and how we were sending our soldiers over there to fight. Again, I truly didn't comprehend the situation or the implications, but I just knew we were going to war and that some of my friends would be leaving to fight.

During my junior year, I was elected sergeant at arms for student council. My responsibility was to instill school spirit and oversee our ticket program. The program involved student council members patrolling the halls between classes, handing out tickets for violations of acting out or talking. The student then had to attend a court to be issued her punishment. The most common punishment was writing an essay on some random topic. The halls of our school were pink, and every graduate had the honor of having her picture hang on one of the school's walls. We loved to look at the pictures of the teachers who had attended Holy Angels and were now nuns. It was funny to see them without their habits. Many of my friends and fellow students' mothers were also on the wall.

My mom got pregnant the summer before my senior year. She waited until she couldn't hide it any longer before she told Barb and me. Barb and I screamed with delight and excitement. Mom was relieved because I think she feared we would be embarrassed. Our baby sister was born in October. Mom and Dad let us pick out her name as long as it was within reason. We wanted a boy, but Mom and Dad really didn't want to raise a son with five older sisters. They were relieved when Pam was born.

Sex? What's that? Mom didn't talk about the subject at all. Sometime during my high school years, she played a record that the mothers in our church community passed around. I don't remember much about what it said, except some little girl saying, "Oh, how gross!" Our principal gave us a talk. She said if there ever was a severe emergency and we *had* to sit on a boy's lap, we had to place a phone book between us—or it was a sin.

One day during my senior year, we heard that the assistant pastor of the church was coming to talk to us about sex. He was a strange man who had previously made advances toward one of our friends. Occasionally, he would teach us our religion class. For the talk about sex, we had to swear that we wouldn't tell the younger students what the topic was. We could hardly wait for the day.

On the day of his lecture, he merely showed slides! It was a joke. He showed us chickens and dogs having sex. When it finally got to humans, the slideshow portrayed a man and woman lying in bed flat on their backs next to each other with sheets up to their necks. Boy, did we get educated that day. We've laughed about that presentation for many years.

But there weren't many opportunities to meet boys at an all-girl high school. There were other high school dances we could attend, but it was intimidating for me since I didn't really know anyone. I was very insecure about my looks. What teenage girl isn't? The icon of the 1960s was Twiggy. It was all about long straight hair, tallness, and extreme thinness. Most of my friends were taller than I and wore this fashion of the day. At 5'1", I had an appropriate weight for my size when I reflect back. Some might have said that I was a little on the heavy side, but that assessment was more indicative of the fashion views of the day. (I also wore glasses until my junior year and had braces. I have had friends experience laugh attacks from seeing photos of me with my glasses from freshman year. We've all seen them. My glasses remind me of the old cars with the big fins coming off the back fenders—only these are coming off the sides of my face. Thank God that I returned from summer vacation before my junior year with contacts and no braces.)

Time passed fairly quickly, and before I realized it, we had graduated. In grade school, I always had thought that I wanted to be a nun, but I think that's a dream of many young Catholic girls. After high school, my dream was to be an airline stewardess and get married. I wasn't so keen on having kids, though. I thought I might want to have children one day, but it wasn't a burning desire. If it happened, it happened; if not, then I thought I could deal with it. One of the requirements to apply to be an airline stewardess was you had to have either two years of college or two years of work experience. I decided to attend a community college and take secretarial courses.

During this time, my Aunt Marge became very sick. Through the years, she had illnesses, but as kids we didn't really understand it all. Then she needed a mastectomy. I remember going to her house to visit with her. She would sit with a pillow on one side to compensate for the loss, popping her bubble gum and blowing bubbles in an effort to quit smoking. Before long we naturally understood that Marge was very ill without Mom really telling us. She died the summer after we graduated high school. The devastation to our family was unreal, the funeral almost unbearable. You could hear the sobbing throughout the church. I'd never seen so many people at a funeral before. Marge touched so many friends. She constantly helped other people. I remember her incredible sense of humor and the laughter she brought to the room. Every year she sent out notes shortly before her birthday to remind her friends.

Marge was a devout Catholic and prayed to the Virgin Mary for everything. She had the words to the mealtime prayer "Grace" painted on her kitchen wall above the dining table. As you looked from our kitchen window inside her home, you would see this painting. After she passed away, I had such an empty feeling to look over at her home and not see her. Our family was devastated for ourselves and for her family. I know my mom lost her best friend, and it was an extremely difficult time for all of us. I still think about my mom and Marge, their relationship, and the love of family, church, and the incredible friendship they shared.

* * *

During the summer after graduation, a high school friend wanted me to come to her apartment for a small party. She and her sister had some friends from out of town over, and they didn't have the right boy-girl ratio. I went with a friend. After we arrived, they asked if we would like a beer. We couldn't believe it. A beer! We decided to split one.

There was one guy, Joe, who kept looking at me and talking to me as if he might be interested. He was the boyfriend of one of the other girls, so I didn't quite know what to do. When it came time for us to leave, Joe said he would take us home. To my amazement, he asked me for my phone number. I couldn't believe he was interested in me. I didn't have a clue if anything would come of it, but it did boost my morale. As we left the party, a boy was walking into the apartment, and Joe said he was one of the other girls' boyfriend. I still can remember what he looked like and how he walked and brushed his bangs with his hand, never dreaming what an important person he would later become in my life.

A month or so later, Joe called. He had just returned from his yearly National Guard training. During our conversation, he asked me out. I couldn't believe it. He was actually serious about seeing me again. I asked about his girlfriend, and he said they had broken up and that it hadn't been serious anyway. I was excited about my new freedom. I had my first full-time job—and now a new boy in my life.

Our first dates blend together in my mind. We went to his mother's house once and just talked. We went to a drive-in, and I was nervous about what he would expect from me. He kept trying to kiss me, and I didn't know what to do. It was evident that he was way out of my league. After all, he was two years older than I was and, obviously, way more experienced. I was so happy that someone was interested in me. But after a few months—before I knew it—we were "doing it." Wow, I had a boyfriend!

I liked Joe a lot. I could easily talk to him, and I didn't have to pretend to be something I wasn't. He gave me the freedom to be myself when I was with him, and I always felt comfortable around him.

Joe moved into an apartment with a friend from work named Roger. Roger happened to be the same boy I saw entering the apartment at the party the first night I met Joe. Their apartment was a half mile from the community college I would be attending in the fall. Joe and I double-dated with Roger and his girlfriends on numerous occasions. We snow skied and attended parties together. I always liked Roger. What Joe lacked in outgoing personality, Roger had in abundance.

* * *

My first day at college, I ran into my high school friend Sandy. We had been very close our senior year. We hadn't realized we were both going to the same college as we hadn't spoken since graduation. That first day, Sandy met Ron, who soon would become her main man. They were acquaintances from grade school. Ron turned out to be one of the greatest friends I would ever have. It wasn't long before we were a threesome. When I wasn't on a date with Joe, I was hanging out with Sandy and Ron, or we were all hanging out together.

Soon, Joe and I were in an on-again, off-again relationship. We had gone to a few parties where he completely ignored me and started flirting with other girls. We had arguments about it. I was getting asked out frequently, and I knew Joe dated other people. We would break up and then one of us would call the other, and—just like that—we would be on again. There was just something about us. We couldn't stay away from each other even though we knew we might break up again. He would treat me terribly, so then I would tell him about dates I had been on. Joe had really seductive eyes, and I melted every time I was with him. If we hadn't seen each other for a while and he called, I would try to build up my resolve. I would tell myself, "Okay, I'll see him, but he'll never get me into bed." The road to hell is paved with good intentions.

When I saw Veronica at school she was engrossed with her nursing courses. We had totally different goals, and I soon learned what college was all about for me. No one cared if you skipped class! I started out with a great attitude, but college was way above me. Biology—what was that? Accounting—well, we all knew how good I was at that. I was the only girl in my business law class. I could go on and on. College just didn't work out for me, but socializing in the pub and playing cards with boys—these were areas where I really did fit in well. There were boys and more boys, and some boys became good friends. Most of my friends from Holy Angels had the same experience at college. After our four years of isolation at the all-girl Catholic school, we went crazy. I had some of the best times of my life during my first year of college—and some of the most stressful as I worried about getting pregnant.

I feel that I need to explain why I did not consider birth control as an option. Since it was a mortal sin to even think about sex, it didn't even enter my mind to seek birth control. If you went to a doctor, you were admitting that you were planning to have sex. Each time I had sex, I told myself it wasn't going to happen again. It would be so embarrassing to go to a doctor for that reason, let alone plan for the inevitable. We just played with fire, hoping and praying pregnancy wouldn't happen.

* * *

In 1967, the Vietnam War became a large part of our lives. So many boys struggled to keep their grades up to avoid the draft. My friend Maria had a boyfriend, Steve, who went to fight in Vietnam. Maria was Veronica's best friend, and Steve asked Veronica to take care of Maria while he was gone. One day Veronica and Maria were out for Chinese food, and Maria's fortune cookie read, "Bad news from overseas." Maria said, "Oh my God,

Steve's dead." Veronica slapped her. When Maria got home, there was a message for her that Steve had indeed been killed. Everything about the war started to hit home, and suddenly life became so complicated. Our carefree days vanished. Every night we watched on the television news as coffins were unloaded from planes. Tragically, Steve died on January 12, 1968, only a few days before he was supposed to come home.

At the end of our first year of college, Sandy confided in me that she was pregnant. We sat at a hamburger joint talking and listening to the radio and the song, "Yummy, Yummy, Yummy" came on. We didn't know whether to laugh or cry, so we did both. Needless to say, Sandy's folks were very upset. They visited a home for unwed mothers and consulted their parish priest for help in figuring out what they should do.

Ron wanted to marry Sandy, but she was too distraught to decide what would be best. She was very much in love with him, but many people were pulling her in different directions. She felt totally confused. The priest refused to perform a ceremony because he said that the marriage would never succeed and that they were too young and didn't understand what they were doing. Soon, Sandy wouldn't even speak to Ron. Ron asked me to help him figure out a way to get Sandy to at least talk to him. All I could think about was how good they were together. I knew Sandy would be a great wife, and I absolutely adored Ron. In my heart, I just knew it would work despite the odds. After Ron was finally able to persuade Sandy to talk to him, they decided to just get married despite what their parents thought. In those days, it wasn't that unusual to get married in your early twenties.

We decided the first thing they needed to do was to find a place to live. Once they found a place, they thought their parents would think they were responsible. I went apartment shopping with them. Looking for an apartment was hysterical because we headed to one of the most expensive areas of Seattle first. What did we know? It looked like a great place to live. We got a quick lesson about economics that day. It wasn't long before we were shopping in a less affluent part of town.

Once Sandy and Ron worked together and refused to back down, their parents and the priest relented. I was a bridesmaid at their July wedding. On Ron's birthday in December, Sandy gave birth to a beautiful little boy named Kelly. They lived through some rough times in their small two-room apartment. I grew closer to them during that time, and I loved leaving college to hang out with them at their apartment.

During this time, Joe and I were broken up, but it seemed as though every time he called me I willingly ran back. Eventually, we began to see each other on a regular basis. Some of his friends told me about another girl he was supposedly still seeing, too. When I asked him about it, he reassured me their relationship was completely over.

About this time, I started to apply for a stewardess job with the airline companies. I visited our family doctor to ask him to show me how to stretch so I could make the 5'2" height requirement. The interviews were nerve-wracking. Talk about being on display! You felt as if they scrutinized every tiny aspect of your body. I had three interviews with TWA, so I thought I might have a shot. By my nineteenth birthday, I received the news that TWA had accepted me, although the company didn't yet know where I would train. It was one of my happiest birthdays—I was on top of the world. My life finally had direction.

TWA contacted me to tell me that there was an opening for me in Kansas City. I didn't return to school and was madly trying to get ready to leave for Kansas City. Mom and Barb gave me a going away brunch with all my buddies.

I saw Joe the last night I was home, and we talked on the phone the next day. He couldn't come to the airport to see me off because he had to work, but we vowed to write and talk by phone often. I had mixed emotions about leaving him. After I said goodbye to my family and friends and boarded alone, I felt so strange. They all stood outside waving as I took off. I watched them as they got smaller and smaller till I couldn't see them anymore. Tears streamed down my face. I was excited, sad, fearful, and joyful all at the same time. It was April 1969.

During training, I felt as if I had journeyed back to high school. Girls were everywhere. I lived in an apartment complex with other girls who were in various stages of training. We all rode a bus downtown to the training center. Despite the fun, I had no idea what pressure was until I started this training—everything had to be perfect. There were no Cs—you had to earn As or you went home. My, it was amazing what I could do when I wanted something badly enough and when I applied myself.

The TWA training went beyond knowledge and understanding; there were severe physical demands as well. During my interview, one of the TWA interviewers told me that I would have to reduce the size of my calves. I don't have small bones and am fairly short, and I have always struggled with my weight. At one point, I weighed 108 pounds, and Mom said I looked sick. My ideal weight was 112 pounds, but that was only three pounds under my limit in training. I constantly worried I wouldn't make a spot weight check. One of my roommates suffered from a water retention problem. Our instructor made an appointment for her to see a company doctor. Before she went to her appointment that afternoon, the supervisors called a spot weight check. She didn't make it, so TWA put her on the next plane home. We couldn't believe it. I learned quickly that there was no leniency when it came to weight.

They also had very high standards of grooming. We had to apply nail polish daily, and lipstick had to be dark enough to see across the room. (The style at the time was white lipstick, so wearing dark lipstick was very strange for us.) Our hair had to be perfectly in place, our clothes impeccable. Unfortunately, I had one disadvantage. One of my fingernails doesn't grow very long due to an injury I sustained when I was a child. I couldn't believe it when a supervisor questioned me about it. I thought that maybe they were taking the rules just a bit too far. However, when we graduated, I received the award for being the "best groomed" of our class, so I guess I didn't do too badly. (I also scored the quickest time for opening up the plane door blindfolded in case of an emergency.) I had found what I knew I would love to do. I was extremely motivated to succeed.

As incredible as it seems, some girls in training had never flown on a plane before. One day they took us up and rolled over the aircraft, dropped 5,000 feet, and simulated turbulence. Several girls got sick, but no one dropped out of training. I couldn't believe these girls would put themselves through this experience without even knowing if they liked to fly. I had loved flying since I was a child and felt so fortunate I would be able to make it a career.

TWA decided the order in which you were assigned based on your birth date, and you were able to give your first and second preferences of where you wanted to live. Word spread fast that, if you didn't think you could be close to home, it was a good idea to choose Kansas City. At least in Kansas City, you could have an apartment before you graduated from the training program, and we were all familiar with the city. San Francisco was my first choice because it was closer to Seattle, and Kansas City was my second. I got Kansas City.

By the time we graduated, I had already rented an apartment and had partially moved in with my roommates—Bobbie, Karen, and Gail. (Gail was from Seattle, too, and Kansas City was Karen's hometown.) We felt sorry for our friends who stepped off the plane in places like New York without a support system of friends or family.

Before our first flights started, we all received five days off. All I could think about was getting home, visiting my family, friends, Joe, and flashing my new wings around. Gail and I flew together to Seattle, and both our dads met us at the airport with huge smiling faces. They were so proud of us.

While I was home, I acted terribly toward my family. I realize now that I was young and selfish, but my behavior was still inexcusable. All I wanted to do was hang out with my friends. I visited Joe, went to the college, and partied. The lecture I got from Dad on the way back to the airport was well-deserved, and I knew it. Later, I felt horrible—and rightly so. I cried a good portion of the flight back to Kansas City.

During the first months of flying, I spent considerable time close to the phone waiting to be asked out. Luckily, I met some really great people at our apartment complex and made some great friends. One of the bachelors in the complex, Steve, decided he would take care of us. Any time there was a tornado watch, we headed to his apartment to eat and be scared together. Gail and I also became great friends with the couple who managed the complex, Suzy and Rick. Bobbie had a steady boyfriend by this time, and we rarely saw her. Karen stayed very involved in the community since Kansas City was her hometown. Gail and I loved to sit around the pool with our new friends and stay up late watching movies. It was quite a life for a young woman.

The only real problem was that I truly missed the scenery of Seattle. Where were the mountains, rivers, lakes, and all the green trees? There was no water-skiing, snow skiing, beaches, or ocean waves. And the heat was just unbearable to me. I wasn't accustomed to sweating and feeling sticky all at the same time. My heart yearned for the beauty and comfort of Seattle.

In spite of my homesickness, the flying part of my job was fun and remained so. What a great job! Yet, there were times of sadness when we flew with GIs returning from Vietnam. Some would be really happy to be coming home, and others were just filled with sadness. Whenever it was possible, we would try to play cards with them to make their flight go by quickly. The GIs got all the extra meals and all of our attention. So many times I would remember Maria's boyfriend Steve and be overcome with sadness that he would never make the flight home to be reunited with his family and Maria. I also thought of my friend Roger, Joe's roommate, to whom I wrote in Vietnam, and the many others I knew who may or may not return home safely.

Joe and I continued to write and call each other. He decided to drive out with a friend to visit me. I was so excited and couldn't wait for him to arrive. I had the best time showing him around Kansas City. We walked in the parks, visited the shopping centers, watched movies, and swam in the apartment pool. We really started to get closer and even talked about getting married and having kids. It seemed as if we were finally making decisions to spend our lives together. When it came time for them to head back to Seattle, I cried and cried. It was really difficult to see him go.

The next month my mom, dad, and three of my sisters came out to visit. It was a great time, and I took them to see all the tourist places. I finally started to feel like an adult around my parents, and it was a wonderful visit in all aspects. I was beginning to feel as if I were mature and living life as a grown-up.

The following month I didn't have my period. I began to get scared but then rationalized that it probably wasn't too much to worry about because flying can mess up your monthly cycle. After a few weeks passed and it still didn't start, I began to suspect that I might be pregnant. I wasn't too crushed because, in the back of my mind, I believed Joe and I would just get married and everything would work out fine. I called Joe to tell him what I suspected. He seemed surprised but not upset. I was supposed to go see a doctor and let him know the results once we knew for sure. (In those days, the only way to know if you were pregnant was to take a test at a doctor's office. There were no home pregnancy tests or women's clinics that provided free pregnancy tests. It also took several days for the results to come back, so there was definitely a waiting period.) I think that we both were fairly sure that it would be positive. My cycle had always been regular, and I had never been late before. We were neither excited nor upset about the possibility; our attitude was more along the lines of "Okay, what will be will be, and we'll deal with it. If we have to get married, so be it; and if not, then we would wait until I returned closer to home to plan our future together."

A couple days later we talked, but I still hadn't been to the doctor. That's when Joe decided to hit me with the most awful news I could ever imagine. His other girlfriend was also pregnant! I was in shock. I couldn't believe what he was telling me. He got two girls pregnant at the same time! Our later conversations are still a blur to me now. I know that I did a lot of begging. In my mind, I couldn't believe he could marry anyone but me. My whole world was just crumbling around me. Joe said that he had decided to marry the other girl. His reasoning was that I was a lot stronger than she was, and he thought I could handle it much better. Lucky for him I was many miles away, and he didn't have to deal with me other than the phone calls. I was an emotional wreck and cried all the time. I had no idea what I was going to do.

When I saw the doctor he confirmed what I already knew. The visit was so uncomfortable. I could just sense all the nurses knew what was going on. The doctor told me that the best thing to do was to contact the local home for unwed mothers. That was after we discussed my religious beliefs and ruled out an abortion. It wasn't legal then, but I got the impression that, if I had pressed the issue, he would have told me where to go to get one. Later on, one of my friends at the apartment complex, a lawyer, offered to pay for me to go to Europe and get one. But because of my beliefs and those of my family's, it was never a consideration for me.

* * *

I was devastated and my whole world felt shaken. I loved my job and the excitement it brought to my life. I worked so hard to finish my training and reach my goal. The ability to travel all over our country and see so many places was just part of what I loved about flying. I enjoyed breaking out of the traditional mode of early marriage and children—I was independent.

Most of my friends thought of nothing other than finding a husband and then having children. Of course there was college, but only so they could get a job and work till the conventional marriage plans came together. All our mothers were stay-at-home moms. Dads left in the mornings and came home at night for the traditional sit-down dinner with the family. I enjoyed living my life of freedom before settling down. Now I had absolutely no idea of what the future held for me.

My entire neighborhood when I was growing up was made of large Catholic families. We lived just down the street from the Catholic grade school. I babysat for one family with six boys. Another neighbor had eight children. They were all Catholic and attended the same school and the same church. Of course, our family was known for the six girls and the beautiful mother with the lovely voice who attended Mass every Sunday and volunteered wherever she was needed. My mother was a member of the Altar Society, a Brownie and Girl Scout leader, and the carpool driver to birthday parties and sports events. She made cupcakes for the school bake sales and attended parent meetings. We were a model family, and we adored our mother. She and Aunt Marge had been the closest things to sainthood that I knew. Can you imagine causing so much pain and disappointment to a saint? My mother had given me so much, had been the perfect role model—and now I was going to bring her such shame. I couldn't bring myself to tell my family.

I had never even heard of a girl in our neighborhood or any of my parents' friends' children getting into "trouble," as they called it. I only had seen the scenario played out in the movies. I adored the Steve McQueen and Natalie Wood movie called *Love with the Proper Stranger*. They had a one-night stand, and when she got pregnant, they found a way in the end to get together. What a storybook ending. Mine, of course, was not going to have the storybook romance or ending. I couldn't believe it was happening to me. I could have curled up into a ball and never uncoiled. My shame! The thought of bringing such disappointment and grief to my parents was almost unbearable. I continued to just wallow in disbelief. What had I done? Through my grief and shame, I had realized that I was so embarrassed. I showed such a disgusting display of naiveté, ignorance, and complete disregard for responsibility. I felt it all weighing upon my shoulders. I put on a great facade to those around me. They would say, "Oh, isn't this terrible; she's such a nice girl. She's being so strong." But I didn't feel so strong; all I felt were shame and guilt.

Joe and I still communicated; and until the day he got married, I tried to talk him out of it. I visited Seattle for five days, and I was able to spend considerable time at home. I learned my lesson from my previous trip home, and I realized the importance of my family. However, I did meet Joe at Sandy and Ron's apartment. We sat in his car and just talked. We were both a mess. I cried in his arms, and he cried in mine. It didn't change my situation, and the day he got married I was an emotional wreck.

I returned to Kansas City to work. I'm still not sure how I managed to gather myself together to function on my job. The closer I got to showing, the harder it was to keep my weight down. As I walked into operations before a flight one day, a supervisor said, "Let's check your records and see how long it's been since you've been weighed." I died. I was two pounds overweight. She hit the ceiling. She gave me one day to take off the weight. I would be weighed when I returned the next day. She didn't want me to fly, but it was too late to call anyone else in. So off I went. After I checked into the hotel, I changed my clothes and headed straight for a restaurant and ordered the biggest steak and baked potato with all the trimmings. I was still overweight when I returned, but by how much—I can't remember. I wouldn't be surprised if it had been five pounds. That was the end of it—I would be fired.

I made an appointment with one of the supervisors and told her my situation. She wrote out my termination immediately. Once a stewardess became pregnant, that was the end of her career. Finished. Now my world was really shattered. Everything I had worked so hard for was gone. I felt a fool, so very stupid. How could I have done this to myself? The supervisor was extremely nice and wanted to make sure I was going to be all right. I said I had a place to go and knew what I was going to do. There was never any doubt about what I would do. Adoption was the only answer. In 1970, girls just didn't raise their babies alone. I figured I could keep this a secret from my parents since I was so far away.

* * *

Before my last flight I made an appointment to see the administrator of the home for unwed mothers. It happened to be just a mile away from my apartment. The appointment didn't last long. She told me how the program worked. I would spend one night there to see what it was like; then I would stay with a family helping out for a few months and then go back to the home until I delivered. My apartment managers were in the process of adopting a baby, and, when I confided in them that I was pregnant, they took me under their wings. It was Suzy who finally convinced me that I had to tell my parents and helped me realize I was going to need their help even if it were just financial.

And what a phone call that was. I got both my parents on the phone at the same time and broke the news. Mom said, "Of course you will give the baby up for adoption." I said I had already made the arrangements and was well taken care of but that I needed them to know. I can't begin to express how I felt telling them this terrible thing. It's not often you're forced to tell your parents something that you know is going to shatter them. I don't wish it on anyone. I experienced many different emotions through the ordeal, but this was probably one of the worst feelings I had ever had.

For various reasons, my roommates and I had to give up our apartment. Bobbie just moved out, and we never saw her again. Gail got transferred to San Francisco and was really excited. Karen went to live with her mother, and of course I had my immediate plans.

Soon it was time for me to spend one night in the home to see what it would be like. I hated it! I was in a dorm with about six girls between the ages of thirteen and fifteen. At twenty, I felt so out of place. This just couldn't be happening to me. The thought of returning to stay for a few months just seemed unthinkable. I didn't allow myself to dwell on it and concentrated on enduring the one night.

During the final month before moving out of my apartment, I spent considerable time babysitting for the managers' new baby girl. I sold some of my clothes to Suzy since I could use the money and she had admired some of my outfits. I wouldn't need them for a while anyway. Steve, the bachelor, would pay me to clean his apartment after a party. I would clean his place while he was at work. When he arrived home, we would cook dinner and watch TV. My friends at the apartment were so nice to me, and I was always included in the parties. It meant so much to me to be included in the usual social life. I felt as though all other aspects of my life and previous comforts were now gone forever.

While I was pregnant, I received a phone call from Joe's new wife. She had had a miscarriage and begged me to let them have my baby. I wasn't interested in that arrangement at all. I knew she was experiencing a tremendous loss, but my mind was made up that I would not let the baby go to them. The thought of someone I knew taking him was not an idea I could even consider. Everything was done so secretively in those days.

When I was about five months pregnant, I moved into a home where I was to be taken care of by a family until it was time to transition into the home for unwed mothers. Rick drove me to my new home. The owner was in the process of getting a divorce from her husband and had just started a new job. Three of her four children were in grade school; the youngest was about three years old.

I couldn't believe how huge and beautiful the house was. It had spacious rooms with gorgeous woodwork inside and was set back on a beautiful yard that seemed to stretch on forever. In the back of the house at the end of the kitchen was the maid's room. This room was now mine. I had my own bathroom next to the bedroom. I was responsible for preparing all the meals and doing light housework. The owner had a maid come in once a week to do the heavier work. It wasn't long before the maid and I became good friends. She was a lovely woman who was always so concerned for me. I got along well with the all of the kids except one little boy. We seemed to clash, so I just tried to stay out of his way; he avoided me as well. I was fortunate for the opportunity to live in such a nice environment. I didn't work on Sundays and spent most of the day in my room. Sometimes I would walk the two miles to church. I didn't go to church while I was flying, but now it seemed familiar and comforting.

I became a pretty good cook while I was at the house because the mother wanted full-course meals all presented in serving dishes. This meal preparation was foreign to me because at home we simply placed the pans on the table. I also had to wash all the dishes. I really enjoyed cooking and trying new recipes for cookies, cakes, pies, and anything else I might like to experiment with. I simply called the local market to order the week's groceries that the mother and I had planned the previous night. Of course, my weight continued to go up and up.

* * *

I didn't want to call my parents for money. They sent some, but I had bills that I couldn't pay. They didn't know about the money problems I had, and this caused me even more stress. One roommate left me with a large long distance telephone bill. Earlier I had purchased some china, and now I couldn't pay the installments. Phone calls to creditors were extremely difficult. I should have asked for help, but I didn't and tried to work it out myself. I thought everything I went through was my punishment for being a bad girl. I deserved it all. The guilt I continued to feel brought more sadness to my life.

Every few weeks I traveled to the home for unwed mothers to see my doctor. I absolutely loved her. She was so short at four foot seven that, when I had my feet in the stirrups, I couldn't see her and could only hear her quiet, accented voice. She had been a doctor in India, where she married an American and moved to the States. She interned at the hospital a half block from the home. She was very sweet and kind. I was fortunate to be surrounded by people so kind and loving.

On one of my doctor visits at the home, I saw a priest for counseling. He wanted to know how my parents were handling my pregnancy. I told him that they weren't handling it very well. I had spoken with Barb, and the things she told me made me feel terrible. Mom was distraught. She and I never talked about my condition except to make sure that I was healthy. The priest suggested that I write Mom and refer to this baby as her grandchild. I did this and soon found out from Dad what a big mistake that had been. In her mind, I should remove myself from being the baby's mother. As a consequence, my mom removed herself as grandmother. I once again felt awful; whenever I thought about it, I would feel sick. I had done the wrong thing again! My mother was experiencing more grief because of me. How could that priest have been so wrong?

During one of my first trips to the home they had given me a battery of psychological tests, and it was time to find out the results. I was upset that I even had to complete them. The tests implied that, because I was pregnant and unmarried, I might be crazy. I resented it. The tests didn't tell me anything revealing about myself. One test was entirely about my parents. I couldn't answer any of the questions, which was when I realized I didn't really know my folks. The test showed that they were perfect, and the psychologist was upset at me. Looking back on it, I'm not surprised. I didn't really know my folks. What kid truly does? My children today know much more about me than my sisters and I ever knew about our parents.

At Christmastime, the woman I worked for decided to throw a party for some friends and their children. It was to be on a Sunday, so I was relieved and thought I could spend the day in my room. I soon discovered that she wanted my help along with the maid's. I felt on display. Her friends had heard about me, and some, I'm sure, could hardly wait to meet "the unwed mother"—or so I thought. It was uncomfortable, but I really had no other choice. Looking back, I'm sure that most of my discomfort was from the shame I felt and that the others were probably not judging me as much as I sensed. It was a very awkward situation for me.

My friends from the apartment were so great, never forgot to visit, and included me in their plans. They would pick up this fat thing (how I saw myself at the time) and take her to a bar, movie, or party. They were my salvation. Karen came over and brought me a Christmas package. It was very sweet. My mom sent yarn and a pattern so I could knit an afghan. Barb had sewn a much-needed maternity dress for me.

I had told a few friends back home that I was pregnant, but I hadn't told Veronica yet. She still talks of that day. She was lying on her bed with her weeks-old baby girl. She begged me to reconsider keeping mine. She promised she would help any way she could. I knew she meant every word that she said. I tried to make her understand that if I kept my baby, then I would never be able to return to Seattle. I couldn't bring that much shame upon my family, and the thought of staying in Kansas City and raising a baby by myself was totally unthinkable. It just wasn't done in those days. Adoption was really my only option.

Christmas passed uneventfully, and it came time for me to move to the home and wait for the arrival of my baby. I was really sad to leave this comfortable existence and move to the home I hated. The only good thing, I would rationalize, was that my stay at the home meant I only had a few months left of the situation.

Once I arrived at the home, I discovered I had some good fortune. I couldn't believe it. I had a small room across from the cafeteria, with only one other girl in it, and we had our own bathroom. My roommate was only sixteen years old, and according to her, she had only had sex once. We got along great, and she seemed very mature for her age. This scenario was very different from my first visit.

Every girl in the home had a job, and I quickly put in to work in the cafeteria. It was very hard work cleaning up after all the meals. By this time, I was getting pretty big. My feet were so swollen that I couldn't fit into any of my shoes. I couldn't find any shoes in the stores to accommodate my poor fat feet, and I wore slippers most of the time.

They prepared us for childbirth by showing us a movie of a birth that took place in the backseat of a car. They had an exercise class, but no one was serious about it. There was no talk of fitness or preparing your body for this ordeal. All the girls talked about was getting it over with, and they even joked about coat hangers and throwing themselves down the stairs.

They soon found work for me in the laundry room sitting down folding towels due to my water retention problems. I was relieved, and it was a much easier job. There were many restrictions on the girls who lived at the home. Most of the girls had come from another city far away. They couldn't go out often, and their trip always had to be supervised. Since I was older and it didn't make any difference if I were seen pregnant walking the streets, they left me alone for the most part. I had to have permission, but I could come and go as often as I liked. Suzy and Rick would take me to their home to babysit or for an evening of dinner and visiting.

On one end of the home was the dormitory; the hospital was on the other end. When you went into labor, you just walked to the other side of the building to deliver your baby. At the home, I became friends with one of the nurses. When she wasn't busy, we would sit for hours in the evening and play cards. We had a little table set up at the end of the hall near the nurse's station. Just the interaction with someone close to my age greatly improved my spirits.

I celebrated my twenty-first birthday in the home—just five days before my due date. I was pretty depressed to be turning twenty-one in a home for unwed mothers. Welcome to adulthood! The housemother and some of the girls gave me a party. The housemother knitted me some much-needed slippers. One of my friends from the apartment came and took me to a tavern. I couldn't believe he would want to be seen with me in my condition, and I could never express how much I really appreciated being taken out for my birthday.

* * *

The rule in the home was that you could only hold your baby once. Some of the girls decided they wanted a meeting with the administrator to try to get the rule changed. The girls wanted me there since I was one of the oldest. The meeting didn't go very well, and the administrator wasn't about to budge. I stayed pretty quiet. I had been around the hospital enough to know that when the nurses got busy you could go into the nursery and hold your baby while they never knew. Besides, I didn't want to rock the boat. I had a good thing going. The administrators left me alone to do what I wanted. They had enough to do with keeping track of the high-school-age girls and making sure they did their homework and chores.

One night as I prepared for bed, the labor pains began. I waited it out for a while until I realized that this must be it. I went upstairs to the hospital. Thank goodness my nurse friend was on duty. It was a terrible night. I was placed in a small room with two beds. The nurse would check on me from time to time and tell me how well I was doing. One of the other girls went into labor that night too, and she was given the other bed. The farther into labor we both got, the louder this girl became. The nurse would come in, and I could hear the girl ask why I was so quiet. Remember, suffer in silence. They wheeled the other girl into the delivery room long before me, and I can still hear her screams. I couldn't believe she was in the delivery room before me.

The nurses took me into the delivery room about 7:30 AM. I was in so much pain but thrilled this ordeal would be over soon. They let us have one person with us, so my roommate came with me. She was great. The nurses kept saying "a half hour more and then this will be over." The baby was turned the wrong way, so they bound my stomach and left me for what seemed like an eternity. Pretty soon they gave me morphine to help ease my pain. My roommate gave me gas, and I kept begging for more, but she had to wait some predetermined time between doses. I thought I screamed when they cut me because I could feel everything. My darling nurse said that I didn't scream, but I think she said that so I wouldn't feel bad.

Finally at 11:10 AM, Michael James was born at eight pounds, fourteen ounces. I remember it was really quiet at first; they kept yelling at him to cry; and finally, he did. I was so out of it that I didn't even ask to see him. I slept the next day, and then they brought him to me. He was so alert and cute; he looked just like his father.

I grew seriously ill. My fever spiked at a very high temperature, and they didn't want me to get out of bed. I could hardly wait to walk down the hall to see how much weight I had lost. When I finally could get down the hall and weigh myself, it was such a big disappointment. I had only lost the weight of the baby. As soon as I could, I called Mom, Dad, and Joe to let them know Michael was born. They were short calls, as I couldn't be out of bed for very long and the phone was located at the other end of the hall.

In the other bed in my room was a sweet sixteen-year-old girl who gave birth to a tiny, precious baby girl. She and her boyfriend were still together, and they agonized over the decision to give up the baby. His family came to see her and brought cute little baby clothes. They were trying to talk her into keeping the baby. I felt so sorry for her and irate at this family for putting her through this. She was visibly upset and torn about the decision.

We could see the babies through the window into the nursery whenever we wanted. When the nurses got busy with a delivery, we would rush into the nursery to hold and feed them. I would stand and look at Michael with so many emotions racing through my body. "This is my baby. No, it isn't. You have no right to feel these feelings. Yes, I do." I felt as if I were on a seesaw, teetering back and forth between having and giving up these yearnings and instincts that I had no experience in understanding.

The days after Michael was born were a blur. Suzy came to visit, and the nurse brought Michael in so she could see him. Another day one of my roommates came with her boyfriend. We had a little room at the end of the hospital hall with a back door. They brought a six-pack of beer, and we sat in that little room visiting and drinking. I think my nurse friend knew what we were doing, but she left us alone. I was in the hospital for about two weeks. Usually the girls left the home before their babies. Since I was so sick, I was still in the home when they came to take Michael away. I was living in my room downstairs when the nurse asked me if I wanted to see him before he left. I went upstairs the next day at the specific time she told me. I dressed Michael, walked him to the back door, kissed him, and said goodbye. I gave him to the foster parents, never dreaming I would ever see him again. I sat in that little back room and cried for what seemed like hours. The nurse came to check on me and offer me some comfort, but in the end, she knew I just needed to be alone in my grief. The tears kept flowing until there weren't any left.

Right up until this moment I somehow seemed to stay detached from the situation. It was almost as if I were watching someone else experience this tragedy. I lived in a dazed existence. My communication home was very limited. On one occasion, before I gave birth, I talked to Barb for about an hour on the telephone. Apparently, Mom and Dad had gone out for the evening. Later, I heard they were really upset with Barb and me for talking for such a long time. They believed I should be spending my money on more important things than a phone call. They had no idea how badly I needed emotional support. That call to Barb lifted me up in a time of despair, but I remember feeling guilty that she received the lecture for my call.

* * *

The home allowed me to recuperate for longer than was usual. Karen came and took me downtown to the county courthouse. The office where mothers place their babies up for adoption was located on the same floor as the office where adoptive parents filled out their paperwork. When I got off the elevator, I saw adoptive parents receiving their babies for the first time. I really just felt as though I were walking through the motions without understanding my surroundings. The social worker took me into a room with a dozen people seated around a U-shaped table. I had to swear that no one forced me into this decision. There were many papers and forms that needed to be completed and signed. One set of papers was for the birth father. I thought all along that I would be honest about everything. Many girls would not disclose the father's name, but I wanted to give my baby the best possible start in life. I wanted all the records to be exact and truthful to the best of my ability. I had to swear that the birth father's signature was truly his. What a difficult day. But it became just another painful memory to endure like so many before. And I knew there would be many more to come.

After I finally left the home, Karen and her roommate graciously let me live with them until I could fly home. I slept on an army cot in their living room and spent my days reading and watching TV. I carried a pillow to sit on with me everywhere because I was so sore. I only ventured from the apartment to go to the store. I didn't have much of an appetite, and I practically lived on vegetables.

My social worker called one day to tell me about the family who received Michael. She said they were young, and this was their first child. It sounded like the home matched up this couple perfectly with Michael. His new dad was a pilot in the military, and his mother was a hairdresser. She was short like me. I had requested just two things for Michael—that he be raised Catholic and that his parents tell him he was adopted. The social worker assured me they would honor my requests.

One day Mom called and pleaded with me to talk to Barb. She wanted me to tell Barb to marry her boyfriend as soon as possible. Mom was understandably anxious. She was concerned that Barb and her boyfriend, Don, were getting too serious and that she would get pregnant. They were both nineteen at the time, and I'm certain Mom feared having two out-of-wedlock pregnancies in her family.

Every week I called home to update Mom on how much weight I had lost. Once I called to ask if I could now come home. Her answer was not yet—just a few more pounds. Then out of the blue, she called to say that I could come home whenever I could arrange travel plans. I was ecstatic, and it only took a few days to get ready.

I was so excited I didn't sleep the night before my flight. I washed and set my hair the night before and was disgusted when I took out the curlers the next morning and my hair was still wet. I wanted to look my best as I walked off the plane. Karen took me to the airport, and we said a heartfelt goodbye. I didn't know if I would ever see her again, and it was so sad for me. She cared so much for me throughout my ordeal.

Once on board, I was really very nervous—nervous about returning to Seattle, how my family would receive me, and returning to a new life. It seemed as though we flew forever. As I walked off the plane, there stood Mom, Dad, and Barb. I burst into tears. I was so excited to finally be back home. My youngest sisters didn't know I was coming home, and the look on their faces when they came home from school was priceless.

* * *

The story we told everyone about my early return to Seattle was that I had a water retention problem in the Kansas City climate, and I decided to come home to try another airline. I was going to look for airlines that actually flew to Seattle, as TWA did not.

Mom and I never spoke of my pregnancy. It was as if nothing had happened. Things carried on as normal. We were all conditioned to act as though nothing had happened, and we did. Again, suffer in silence and never speak of it to anyone. I thanked God I had my friends to talk to and confide in. Sandy and I hashed the whole thing over, and I told her all the gruesome details. She was very sympathetic and understanding and let me cry and talk as long as I needed.

The home told us that we would eventually forget our babies in time. There would come a day when we would even forget their birthdays. They said that, as we had other children, the new baby would replace the void left by the child we lost to adoption. Over and over, we were told that we had to have loved our babies greatly to have given them up. However, I looked at it as a cop out—the "easy" way out—and felt horrible about it. I believed I was a coward. The hard thing would have been to keep him.

From all of the conversations I then shared with Barb, I began to realize how upsetting the whole ordeal had been for Mom. After listening to her explain what went on while I was gone, I just didn't feel I could bring the subject up to my mother. I wasn't about to initiate a conversation about a subject that distressed her so much. I figured that, if she wanted to know any detail, she would ask me. After all, she was the mother, and I was still the child. That was how I viewed our relationship.

The second day after I arrived home I spent the afternoon with Joe. We were both so sad and talked about my experience with Michael. Joe dropped me off at Veronica's house for a visit, and then later she took me home. She was so upset about what had happened and still couldn't believe that I had to give up Michael.

I also visited with Roger, and by the third night we decided to go out. I hadn't seen him since he had been in Vietnam. He knew about my pregnancy, as Joe's wife told him at a party one night. I was upset that she told him, but I suppose he was eventually going to find out. Roger and I were good friends and kept in touch. I knew all his old girlfriends since we often double-dated when Joe and I were together. Anytime we experienced boyfriend or girlfriend problems, we would talk to the other person about it. It seemed so natural to go out as friends, catching up on the last few years' events. He listened to my story and was so kind, and I listened as he detailed his years in the service.

A few months later, we heard that Joe's wife was pregnant. Roger and I continued to see each other although it no longer was merely friendship. I was drawn to him because he had a great sense of humor and an engaging personality, and he knew exactly what he wanted in life. He was very ambitious, attending school and working full-time.

It was so different to date after I came home from Kansas City. Mom sat up nights waiting for me to come home. I tried to alleviate her fears by explaining that I was on the pill. She still seemed worried. Even though

Roger and I weren't having sex—it was way too soon for that—I didn't want her to worry. Roger shared an apartment with a friend. Sometimes we would get involved talking with friends, and I felt too old to say I had to be home by a certain time. Every night I would go out, my mom would sit in her chair waiting for me to come home. I would just die when I could see her from outside the window. I just couldn't take any more of her lectures.

I got a job as quickly as I could find one so I could move out. Dad helped me find a car. One of my flying buddies needed a roommate, and before long, I was able to put everything together so I could be on my own again. Much to my mother's delight, Barb and Don got married right after Don's twentieth birthday. I suppose my talk helped out a bit. The wedding was a joyous occasion for our family, and marriage seemed so natural for Barb and Don. We all adored Don, and they seemed absolutely right for each other.

One day Roger told me about some upcoming parties for his company. He wanted me to go, but he knew Joe and his wife would be there. (Roger and Joe still worked together at the same place.) Roger asked me if I wanted to go or if he should even be asking me. I couldn't bear to think of him asking someone else, so I told him to ask me. We went to the parties, and I just tried to stay away from Joe and his wife as much as possible. At one of the gatherings, it was especially difficult because Joe and his wife brought their new baby girl. Fortunately, I could stay far enough away, so I didn't have to see the baby. By this time, everyone knew Roger and I were an item, and Joe pretty much left me alone. Joe and I were cordial to each other, but we didn't have any real conversations.

About this time, I realized that I was very serious about Roger. It was inevitable I would run into Joe from time to time, so I decided to just grin and bear it. Roger was very sympathetic about it and watched out for me as best he could. It certainly wasn't easy, but as time wore on, I began to heal.

Roger and I dated for about a year when we decided to go on a vacation together. I told Mom because I knew I wouldn't be able to keep it from her. I didn't want to hide it behind her back. I planned to be out of town for a week, and I wasn't going to lie to her. Going on vacation with my boyfriend certainly wasn't the right thing to do in her mind, but she realized that I was on my own and that I was going to do as I pleased. My mom decided to ask why we didn't just make it a honeymoon.

I was a little taken aback by her question, but I knew in my heart that Roger was "the One." There was absolutely no doubt he was the man I should marry; it seemed so right. At a subconscious level, I think getting married and planning a family would make me legitimate. I had to set my life right, especially in Mom's eyes. I could recall remembering the details of the first time I saw Roger—how he walked and how he brushed his bangs to the side with his hand. Shortly into our relationship, we even had discovered that we had played together as children. He grew up five doors down from my grandparents' house, and his mother worked with my grandfather. This seemed to be just another sign that he was the man for me.

Everyone liked Roger. We had many great times with Sandy and Ron, and they now were his friends too. He got along with my all my friends. He truly made them his own as I had done with his. I approached Roger with Mom's plan; with some hesitancy, he agreed. Truthfully, I guess you could say I proposed to him. We had dated for a year by then. I felt certain in my heart, so I tried to make him see it as well. He finally did. Years later, however, he confessed that he had decided to go along and just marry me—knowing that, if it didn't work out, we could always get a divorce. We have laughed about his confession many times during our thirty-seven years of marriage.

As was the company custom, we sent a wedding invitation to the office. As I was getting ready for the ceremony, Barb relayed that Joe and his wife were there. She thought Dad saw him. I was incredulous—I could not believe they would come to my wedding! I refused to dwell on it, though. I put it out of my mind, walked down the aisle, and enjoyed my wedding day to the fullest. After that day, I barely even looked at him at other company functions.

* * *

Roger and I led a great married life. We bought a little three-bedroom brick house. After Roger graduated from college, we traveled to Europe with our good friends for three weeks and then later drove to Kansas City to visit some of Roger's relatives. His parents were originally from Missouri. I enjoyed showing Roger around town. To my amazement, I found the home for unwed mothers—it had become a home for disabled children—and I recognized the place where I lived and took carc of thc kids.

Coincidentally, I discovered that Roger was adopted. I don't remember when I found out, but it was as if I had always known. His adoptive father died when he was only ten years old; his mother raised him by herself with no other relatives living in Seattle. It seems so strange to me now, but Roger and I never talked about his being adopted. We rarely spoke of Michael, either. I was conditioned not to think about him. I never forgot his birthday, but I didn't dwell on it. Barb, Sandy, and Veronica always remembered the birthday with me. I think they hurt right along with me every time the day passed on the calendar.

Two years into our marriage, I decided it was time to have a baby. Roger was not very crazy about the idea but finally agreed. I was very ready, but the only thing that scared me was the delivery. Roger asked his mom about his adoption because we were having children and would like to know any pertinent medical history. She absolutely fell apart, crying and carrying on about her miscarriages; she was unwilling to talk about any of it. So that subject was permanently dropped.

It was relatively easy for me to get pregnant. I came from fertile stock, as my sisters and I often joked. I was thrilled about having a baby while

Roger was a little apprehensive. Since he was raised an only child and didn't have any cousins, he hadn't been around babies at all. We were in the middle of fixing up a rental home we purchased for an investment, so I spent the summer pregnant and working on this rental property. We paid my sisters to help us get it painted and rented. We had a fantastic summer doing that, and I had so much fun with my younger sisters now that they were teenagers. Roger really loved my sisters as well.

I was frustrated because most of the friends I knew from Roger's work didn't know or realize that this was my second pregnancy. I would have to sit there very quietly while they would tell me what childbirth was like. I constantly told lies by now. It doesn't make you feel very good about yourself when you are living a lie, but that's how I felt. Years later I found out that many of them did know, but they weren't going to tell me they knew my "secret." It's amazing to think that, back then, the worst thing a man could do was commit murder while a woman's worst offence was getting pregnant out of wedlock.

Soon we moved into a bigger house. A friend from high school, Mary, called out of the blue one day and said that we should get together to catch up. We met for lunch at her house, and it really was like old times. She and another friend had little baby girls while I was pregnant with Julie. (This was another time when I had to listen attentively to someone else's childbirth stories. I never dreamed I could tell them what had happened to me in Kansas City.)

I never imagined I could have such an easy time giving birth to my little Julie. When I went into labor, I was so scared. I couldn't believe it was time to do this again. Much to my surprise, things were totally different. The nurses gave me a drug to help me relax, and I was so relaxed I couldn't answer a simple question. They asked me where we lived, and after trying to get the words out for what seemed like five minutes, I just turned to Roger and said, "You tell her." They wheeled me into the delivery room, and in about fifteen minutes Julie just slid out.

Now, this was just too good to be true. I thought I was dreaming. But no, I had a beautiful little six-pound, four-ounce girl. I never dreamed I would have a girl, as my only experience was with a big boy. I started to realize that my experience with childbirth in the home was a little barbaric by the current day's standards. (Of course, it's even more different today with natural childbirth where many women elect not to use drugs at all. Now you get classes on how to keep your body healthy, as well as breathing exercises and various tips for a more pleasant birthing experience. When I gave birth to Michael "naturally," I had no education or assistance in how to do it.)

Roger turned out to be the best possible father. He loved doing absolutely everything for her, including changing dirty diapers. She had to be powdered just so, and he would exercise her by hanging onto her little hands and raising her up. This was long before I had heard about the benefits of exercising your babies. It was such a joy to watch Roger's transformation into this caring father.

It wasn't too long after we moved in to our new home that Mary called to say that she and her husband were moving in a house down the street from us. Sometimes, those unbearable days with toddlers were made tolerable by our get-togethers. The girls would play together, and Mary and I would watch our soap operas and visit. By this time, I had shared my experience in Kansas City with her. Veronica was living only a mile away from us as well, and Sandy also lived less than five miles away. I was once again blessed with such dear friends. One day, Mary whimsically suggested we get pregnant at the same time. We agreed it was a great idea! I got pregnant right away of course, and Mary got pregnant eighteen months later. To this day, we laugh about it, and my Karen and her Eric are still very close.

We lived some glorious years in our late twenties and early thirties. Sandy had three boys. When Karen was a toddler, Sandy and I started taking the kids up to my family's beach house for a couple weeks during the summer.

Our husbands would come up on the weekends. By now, my folks had replaced the little cabin with a home large enough to accommodate their rapidly expanding family. Having several generations gather under one roof, share meals, and enjoy the beach as our playground has enabled us to become the very close family that we are today. I feel very fortunate to share the beach life with my own daughters.

I am also blessed with some wonderful sisters. Eventually, I couldn't view them as just little kids anymore. They babysat for me all the time. (I never had to hunt for a babysitter.) It was even better when they grew into adult women, and our relationships matured. As a child, I thought that I couldn't experience anything better than the times at the beach. I was wrong, however, because the times we have shared as adults have also been wonderful. We share great times with our children but also savor the times with just the siblings. As the years passed, I became close to Sandy's oldest son, Kelly. He is only one year older than Michael, so I was able to gauge Michael's development through the years by observing Kelly's. Years later, I learned that many mothers who give their babies up for adoption subconsciously find a replacement baby to bond with. Kelly was mine.

When I was pregnant with Julie, Sandy was also pregnant. We were both due in November. At five months, Sandy developed some problems and had to be confined to bed rest. I would go over to fix her lunch and help out with the boys. It was such a difficult time. She had to lie flat on her back and couldn't even sit up a little to eat. In the end, Sandy went into labor prematurely, and it was too soon for a baby to be born in those days. Today with modern technology, the baby might have survived. Their baby was a little girl, and Sandy and Ron named her Mary. What can be worse than a death of a child, no matter what age or how it happens?

Sandy and I have shared special bonds with each other's children. Julie is very special to Sandy because she and Mary would have been the same age. Kelly was my replacement child for Michael. Sandy and

I spent every summer together at the beach for ten years. Sandy's boys and my girls were so much fun to watch growing up together. They were as close as brothers and sisters—but without the fighting. They loved spending time together.

Veronica was a labor and delivery nurse. What is it about nurses? Just saying someone is a nurse says so much about the person. Veronica and I had talked about Michael on numerous occasions. She never could fully comprehend my detachment from the whole matter. One day she looked at me and asked, "When are you going to deal with this subject?" She knew it had become increasingly difficult for me to get through each birthday. I tried to forget, but as I got older, the more difficult it became. About the same time we had this discussion, we saw a Phil Donohue program about adoption. A sixteen-year-old girl sat between her adopted mother and her birth mother. I was in shock. I couldn't believe this could be done. Veronica wanted me to look into it. We fantasized all day about the possibilities.

Veronica also questioned me about my grief. She knew that, when I came home from Kansas City, I was never given the proper opportunity to grieve. She explained to me that what I lost was no less than a death of a loved one. She kept telling me how unhealthy it was to bottle all that up inside and to pretend that it never even happened. It didn't take me long to agree. Yes, I did have a loving husband and two beautiful daughters, but no, I was not okay. I knew it. She gave me the name of a counselor, and I made an appointment.

There were many things emotionally wrong in my life. For the longest time, there was a wall between my mother and me. How could I be close to her when I couldn't share the most tragic episode in my life with her? We got along fine, but there was just something missing in our relationship. I also struggled with sharing my grief with Roger. Sometimes I cried myself to sleep on Michael's birthday. For a long time, I wouldn't tell Roger when it was his birthday, and I just tried to conceal my grief and anguish.

I got to a point where every song on the radio would remind me of my lost child. Once I allowed myself to start thinking about the things I had endured, I really struggled to stop. Thinking about it had a domino effect and set my mind racing uncontrollably. I thought I was going crazy. All the while Veronica kept telling me that these were normal feelings of grief. I didn't think or feel normal, though. The home told us we would eventually forget; with other children, it would erase the memory of the child given up for adoption. I wasn't forgetting, though, and nothing could fill the void left by Michael's absence.

By now Roger had begun a different career. We decided he should try something new, get out of the corporate world, and work for himself. He started selling tools for a large nationwide company. He was a great salesman. One of his coworkers told us about an upcoming self-help seminar. Many of the guys were planning to attend, and we decided it would be a great experience for both of us.

I really was just attending the seminar to support Roger. I didn't realize it might have something to offer me as well. Wow, did it open my eyes! I attended workshops about how you can be anything that you want to be. There were ways to move beyond traumas and negative experiences in your life. They emphasized how experiences, whether good or bad, greatly affect your life and attitudes. It was important to see the value of those experiences, learn from them, and then move on in a more positive way. My new mantra became "Grieve it, and shake it off."

Both Roger and I loved the seminars and made it a central part of our lives. During one of the presentations, I really had an eye-opening experience. I realized I needed to move forward from what I had been thinking about. They taught me that I needed to visualize very specifically about what I wanted. At our beach house, the outside fire pit was the place where we spent most of our evenings when it wasn't raining—hanging out, playing games, making s'mores and telling tall tales. So for me, this is what I envisioned—seeing Michael sitting around that fire pit, with the rest of my family.

I really thought that, at one point, I was basically satisfied with my life. I had two beautiful daughters and a wonderful husband. My goals revolved around keeping my family cared for and happy. But after attending the conference, I realized I had more goals than that the family-oriented ones. I recognized my need to find Michael. I understood it would not be an easy task and, possibly, would not meet the approval of many people. But in my heart, I made it my goal.

I started to attend support group meetings for parents affected by adoption, and I read every book I could find on the subject. Mary went with me to the first meeting. We were amazed at the amount of information available. They told about several reunions and talked about how searches were conducted. One of the first things I learned was that it is very difficult to search for a child who is still a minor. This was 1983 and Michael was only thirteen years old. I struggled with the issue of finding him while he was still that young. Many birth mothers think that it is their duty to search and find their child, even a minor child. I had heard horror stories about children being in an abusive home, or never being adopted—any other horrible situation you can imagine. I became engrossed in exploring every aspect of the subject. Every time I turned around, there would be another talk show about adoption, and I taped them all.

Veronica knew a counselor who worked with people in adoption at a children's home, so I started to see him. It was helpful and encouraging to talk with someone about how I felt. By the end of the sessions, I had made up my mind to begin my search for Michael. I'm not sure the counselor agreed with my decision. Years later, when I saw him at a meeting, he told me he had never counseled a birth mother before meeting me. It gave him a new perspective on birth mothers. I asked him if I should tell my girls about Michael. They were eight and six years old. He told me to wait until my next session, so he could confer with his peers. The next week he said they didn't think it was a very good idea. I was disappointed; I thought the whole point of my getting better relied on my ability to face the truth and stop living a lie. My instinct was that I thought it would be better if my girls grew up knowing, rather than waiting until they were in their teens to spill the news. Who could predict what would happen? What if Michael showed up on our doorstep one day?

After discussing it with Roger, I decided to tell the girls. They were both at a young enough age that I didn't need to go into great detail. I just said that before I married their father, I had a baby boy, which meant they had an older brother. They were naturally surprised but also really excited. They hugged each other, and Julie yelled to Karen, "We have a brother!" Then they hugged each other again. I told them I didn't know where Michael was, and that someday I would find him. The next thing I knew, Karen said, "Mom, what's for dinner?" and that was that.

My instincts were right. As they got older, they had other questions and I answered them as they came up. Karen was the most verbal. She would say, "I hope you find Michael, Mom." I would agree, and then we went on to another subject. My meetings, reading, and talking on the phone to other people affected by adoption simply became a part of our lives.

* * *

After sharing with the girls, I then had to alert many of my friends. I didn't know if the girls would talk about it to their friends, but we needed to be prepared. Barb told her boys, Mary her kids, and Sandy her children. I called Julie's best friend's mother and said, "You better sit down for this one." She was very nice about it and thanked me for warning her. Sure enough, Julie did tell her friend, and then her mom could answer any questions she asked. It was like the cat being finally let out of the bag. I had a few friends who were adoptive parents. I felt that I owed them an explanation before I found Michael—there was so much I needed to answer. They were all very understanding and supportive, at least while they spoke to me. Inside, I'm sure they were conflicted as I certainly would have been.

I found out there was going to be a National Adoption Congress Conference in Seattle in the summer of 1984. I thought that this would be a better way to find out more about everything I needed to know. I called Joe because he had once seemed so interested in searching for Michael, and there were several classes on birth fathers. He never showed up. It was a fantastic conference and I learned so much. I met several other birth mothers who became my friends. We went to meetings together and shared our stories. It was good to talk to women who felt the same way I had and who had had similar experiences.

One woman I met was a searcher in Arizona. One night we were talking about the issue of searching for minors, and she said there were people who would get the information you needed—for a fee. We were truly surprised that these searches were actually done. Roger and I didn't know anything about searching and what actually happens. I came away from the conference excited but also a little disappointed. I found out that Missouri was a closed state, meaning that even if the adoptee was an adult, they would not open the records. We did, however, hear of states being closed and then one day they would open up, so there was a glimmer of hope on the horizon.

After I left the conference, I drove straight to Mom's house and explained to her where I had been and what I had gotten out of it. I left her with the first book I read about adoption, *Lost and Found.* It was considered the Bible for the adoption movement. It was such a relief to break our silence on the subject finally. Mom read the book and recommended it to my sisters. I can't explain the weight that lifted from my shoulders once I could openly talk with all my family about the adoption. Mom and I hashed everything out. When I got home from Kansas City, she didn't bring up what had happened because she assumed I didn't want to talk about it. You never realize how this kind of pent-up stress will manifest itself. For example, for years, I lived with a terrible habit of biting the inside of my mouth. No matter how hard I tried to stop, I just couldn't. A week after I had finally talked to my mom after all those years, I had stopped the nervous biting. My mouth had totally healed.

I proceeded to gather all the paperwork involved in a search. I joined organizations to receive their newsletters, wrote to the courthouse where Michael's files were kept, and contacted the agency I thought might have handled the adoption. I learned that I had a legal right to ask for a copy of any paper I had signed during the adoption process.

At the time, I had never asked any questions or even considered that I had a right to them. The judge at the courthouse responded and said he would add my letter of introduction to Michael to his file so that if he ever requested his records, everything would be released to him. The adoptive parents had moved out of the area, and the agency hadn't heard from them since that time. My biggest disappointment was the agency's refusal to tell me his first name, even though I believed this information would not have violated any confidentiality. However, I had already given the baby the name of Michael at birth. It gave me some comfort being able to call him by a name I chose.

* * *

Roger and I attended another adoption meeting together. By this time, he started to show interest in the topic for himself. He wasn't going to do anything just yet, but he wanted to understand what this was all about and to support me. We got an application for Roger so that if he ever decided to search, then he would have the necessary paperwork. About this time, I heard another rumor about certain records being miraculously opened up for a large sum of money. I was intrigued. We were initially told you couldn't search for a minor, but then I also started hearing stories of minors located … for a price.

I began to truly comprehend how the entire adoption system is an arbitrary bureaucracy. One person decides records should be closed, and someone else decides they should be opened. People's lives were being controlled by others with no sensitivity or concern for those whose emotions and lives they greatly impacted. I learned quickly you had to be very careful if you chose to pay someone to help you in your search. We often heard stories about people paying a detective or someone else to initiate searches only to end up by spending thousands of dollars without any results.

I also began speaking on a weekly basis with a woman I had never actually met in person. I don't know how she got my name, but I wasn't really concerned about it. By this time, I was a member of several adoption organizations and had previously attended many meetings where she might have accessed my name. She was a birth mother who was also an adoptee. She seemed very understanding, and we would talk for hours about the adoption experience. She also had some connections in Missouri where I relinquished Michael.

* * *

One Saturday afternoon, I got a call from a woman who said her name was Susan. She asked me a few questions "to be sure she was talking to the right person." She went on to ask if I were really interested in finding a minor child. Of course, I replied, yes. I was informed it would cost me a large sum of money, but that it was possible. I couldn't believe what I was hearing. She said a man would call me either Monday or Tuesday evening to give me the details and to see if I were truly serious. I ran to the yard where Roger was working to tell him. At that moment I struggled to keep all the thoughts racing through my mind.

We didn't make any decisions one way or the other but just wanted to see what this man would say. Every time the phone rang Monday night, my heart would beat faster. Finally, the call came. He never gave a name. It appeared he was reading the original birth certificate as he had date of birth, doctor, place, time, and weight. The man explained he would place the original certificate in the mail to me. I was supposed to check it over, and if I determined it was the correct one, then I would place $1,000 cash in a brown paper envelope in the mail to a certain PO box. After he received the cash, he would then mail the amended birth certificate that had Michael's adopted name and his parents' names.

I repeated, "Cash?"

"Yes," he replied. "It must be cash." He assured me it wouldn't get lost. I agreed to all of it. If it did come in the next two days, then Roger and I would talk about it. I hadn't made up my mind one way or the other. Did I really want to find Michael this way? The man, of course, emphasized that I wasn't to tell anyone about our arrangement. He specifically stressed not to ever tell Michael's parents. I wouldn't have done that anyway. It would have made me appear a desperate woman, and that was not the image I wanted Michael's parents to have of me.

As I hung up the phone, I was trembling. How could this be happening? What was I going to do if the birth certificate really showed up in the mail? Was this legitimate? Or was this a scam to get $1,000 cash out of me and then return no information? The entire scenario seemed very risky with no guarantee. I really didn't know what to do or how to check it out.

I decided to speak with my friend from Arizona who was more informed about searches, so I called her. She was utterly appalled. She had heard of this kind of search but at a much higher price. At the end of our conversation, she reassured me that she would make a few phone calls, without mentioning my name, to see if she could find anything out for me. My friend didn't learn anything more than I had found out but asked me to let her know when I received the package in the mail.

I waited. Two days went by, and I received nothing. A week passed. Still nothing. Then one day, I went to the mailbox and found the following letter:

April 1985

Janet,

I had a feeling that you couldn't keep your mouth shut when I talked to you on the phone. The information you want is not for sale anymore. You know who got the information plus a whole lot more. Tell all your friends thank you for helping you out. You saved yourself some money, but lost your son again. This time for good.

No signature. I was both devastated and frightened by the tone of the note. I didn't understand how this could have happened. I had only told one person, other than Roger. I tried to sort it out in my mind. What had I done? Their threat of taking my son away, permanently, slowly sunk in. Could they have destroyed my records? From then on, I felt paranoid at every meeting I went to. Did other people know who I was? Veronica and I got together at least once a week, and we would go over and over it. In the end, as I usually do, I tried to look on the bright side. It took quite a bit of work to find the positive side of this experience. If I had my choice, I wanted to find Michael in the "right" way. It looked more and more as though I were going to have to wait until he turned eighteen.

By now, all my family and friends were also dedicated to my search. It was incredible the attitude we all maintained. There was no doubt in anyone's mind that I would find Michael. It was a matter of *when*, not *if*. Sandy and I would dream about Michael visiting the beach with us and playing with Kelly and the other kids. It became more and more apparent that there was a child missing from our lives.

The days, weeks, and months slowly slipped by. Roger became more interested in finding his family. He witnessed what I, as a birth mother, went through and thought maybe his birth mother might be going through the same thing. He also thought, as many adoptees do, that he should wait until his adopted mother passed away before he initiated anything. However, his adoptive mother was soon diagnosed with Alzheimer's disease. Sadly and slowly, she became more of a child than a mother to him. He would bring the issue up occasionally and ask me when I planned to do something about it for him. This kind of annoyed me. Finding a lost relative not only involves someone else searching for you, but you also need to be prepared and informed of the possible outcomes. It not only affects you emotionally, but you also must ask yourself what expectations you have for the person once you find them. You may also need to realize this person could have expectations of you as well. Are you prepared to accept what can happen, either good or bad? At this point, Roger had attended only one meeting and not read any books about reunions or adoption.

While we moved Roger's mom to a nursing facility, we found a letter from her lawyer that told about the agency that handled his adoption. We couldn't believe it was one block away from where Roger was raised and also the same neighborhood in which I had grown up. We felt foolish that it had been virtually in our own backyard the entire time. My counselor worked for the same agency. I called and asked if he could get us any information about Roger's adoption.

The National Adoption Conference was to be held in Boston that year. We thought it was a perfect opportunity to take a needed vacation, and we could attend the convention together. Roger would also get firsthand information on searching for his birth mother. I recorded *Lost and Found* in a tape recorder for Roger to listen to in the car on his daily commute. It took weeks for my counselor to find and get Roger's records, but finally he called. We made an appointment to see him. We couldn't believe the information the counselor had found. Roger's birth mother had named him Stephen. Roger said when he was a little boy he used to have a pet name for himself—Stephen. She kept him for a couple of weeks. Her story so closely resembled mine that, as I heard it, I paced the room in tears. I jokingly said today was the day Roger was born! We received three pages of information on Roger's adoption history. He had been moved seven times before his adoptive parents finally received him at seven months old. The counselor said his mother wasn't from Seattle but from a town close by. We didn't have any identifying information. But what we had was fascinating and intriguing. We finally had some medical background and heritage. Roger was German and Irish, just like me.

We turned in Roger's paperwork to initiate his search and soon they assigned a confidential intermediary (CI) to Roger's case. We met her the summer of 1987. I liked her immediately. Yet, it was incredibly frustrating as we had Roger's original birth certificate information, but she had the amended version. We were not allowed to know anything on it. She did tell us Roger's mother's first name was Rose, and that was some solace. By this time it was starting to sink in. We were actually going to find Roger's family. Periodically, I talked to our CI, but it was a slow process. His birth mother's maiden name was a very common one. She really had to dig to find any information. There were numerous dead ends.

Our CI asked me in early February 1988 how I was proceeding with my own search. I said Michael would be eighteen in March and asked her if there were anything I could do in the meantime. She advised me as to whom I should contact next. At this point, my attitude was that I never really knew if a lead would get me anywhere or not. As far as I knew, Missouri was still a closed state, and it still looked to be a great many years before I found him. I called the number my CI gave me and was referred to a number in Missouri. I called, and the woman I talked to said she could have a name in three days for a fee. I was dumbfounded! Was it really going to be this easy? She said this source had just been made available to her a couple of months ago. Unbelievable! I spent the next hours calling everyone who was in my significant circle. They were all as surprised as I was.

Like so many times throughout this five-year process, I was anxiously awaiting a phone call. I decided my life lesson must be patience. On February 24, 1988, I received my son's name. It is David Michael. I was told that I would be sent the amended and original birth certificates in the mail—immediately! It's so hard to explain the incredible range of emotions I felt just upon hearing these few simple details. I couldn't believe his middle name was Michael. I could still call him Michael and only be half wrong. The mere fact that he was alive was probably the most comforting news of all. You always shield yourself by imagining and being able to accept the worst scenario first and then work your way to envisioning the best outcome if possible. Once again, I called all my significant others. Three days later I received the birth certificate. It wasn't my signature on the original, but that's normal. Next to the word "legitimate" on the original, it said "NO"; on the amended it read "YES."

Julie decided to check the local phone book for the last name even though we doubted they lived in Seattle. Veronica called from work the next day whispering, "David means beloved and Michael means godlike." I called Roger's searcher the next day to find out how I should proceed now. She said I could have an address within three or four days. I just went crazy when she told me that. The searcher tried to relay to me something about Roger's search, but I didn't hear a word of it. Karen had a dentist appointment that afternoon, but I couldn't go into the office with her. My sister Peg went with me, and we just sat in the car and played backgammon to pass the time. I was afraid that if I went into the office with Karen, I would burst into laughter and make a fool of myself; I was so giddy with the news.

Then, I had to endure yet another waiting period. Patience! That Monday I went to Veronica's, and we composed a letter to David's folks. I had made up my mind that I would contact Michael's parents first before I tried to contact him. I wanted to make contact in the most open, honest, and straightforward way possible. I didn't want any more secrets or any sneaking around. Veronica and I wrote the letter in just an hour. She was truly inspired, and it was a beautiful letter. It ended up being a three-week wait before I received the address. In the meantime, another March 8th passed. This was the best birthday for Michael I had ever experienced. No more tears and despair—just pure simple joy! Finally, on March 17, the call came through, and I had an address. Karen ran to get the world globe and encyclopedia to locate the state of Iowa. I made quite a few more phone calls to update everyone on our progress.

David could never know how much he meant to so many people. I've always hoped he could somehow feel the love that was sent his way for so many years. There was a large circle of friends and family who prayed for him, celebrated his birthday, and generally just cared about his well-being.

I asked Julie and Karen if they wanted to write David a letter to be included with mine. Karen started one right away. Julie took her time agonizing over what to say. I told her she didn't have to if she didn't want to, but two days later her composition was finished.

On a Saturday night, we invited friends and a couple of sisters over for dinner. We put all the letters together. There was one to David's parents that explained who I was. At the very least, I asked for some response to my letter and, hopefully, a photo of him. I stated that I realized he was still in school and that, if they decided not to tell him until after graduation, I would understand. I emphasized that I did not want to parent him. I only wanted to ease his mind by sharing with him about his background, medical history, and why I had given him up for adoption. I included the girls' letters, a personal letter to David from me, and some photos. We spent quite some time assembling the package exactly how we wanted it. We wanted David's parents to read my letter first before they found the smaller envelope with the girls' letters and pictures. Before we left the house to go to dinner, we all touched it and sent good vibes. After dinner, we found a mailbox. I stood in front of the mailbox. What a feeling. All this waiting, and this was it. Once I dropped the letter, there was no turning back. I said a prayer and let it fall from my fingers. We went back to the house afterward to play cards—a typical Saturday night activity. I couldn't concentrate on anything as my mind constantly raced. I felt unsettled. Again, another period of waiting. I hoped they would receive the letter on Tuesday. It was a strange kind of limbo. Veronica kept giving me candles to burn. We kept a candle burning for three weeks straight at my house and at hers. Sandy said a novena to Saint Teresa for eight days. Veronica chose to pray to Saint Jude, and I prayed to Mary, Joseph, and Jesus—the ultimate family.

Roger and I decided that maybe the CI should call to see how David's parents handled the news of our search. I really was worried about them. How would I feel if it were me on the receiving end of that packet of letters? It had been three weeks. Veronica agreed to make the call for us. It was Palm Sunday, so Roger and the girls attended church. As soon as they left, I turned on some soft music to meditate. Sweat poured down my body. In the evening, she called to say they were out of town but then added, "Your son has a very nice voice." She talked to *him*! Oh my God! He walks, he talks. I thought I would die!

We decided to try again Thursday night. Veronica and I spent the day together. We went car shopping for her and then returned to the house for the afternoon. She looked at me and said, "I want you to listen to me and not say a word. Just listen to what I have to say." She was very serious. Okay ... I didn't have any idea what this was about. Then she let this one hit me. "I want *you* to make this phone call, not your CI. You are the only one who can do this. This is your search, no one else's. No one can do this for you. Why are you going to let a stranger do this for you?"

Well, I went crazy at her suggestion. "You're kidding, Veronica. Don't make me do this." I started jumping up and down. I paced the kitchen, ranting and raving. I tried to think about everything she had said, and it dawned on me. She was absolutely right. His parents may perceive me as a threat. So, I am the one that needs to talk to David's mother. I realized how right she was. My insides tightened and my palms began to sweat. We read the tarot cards, and it became even clearer. They talked about communication and how I needed to follow my dreams. We knew what had to be done, but it was too late that day. I had to go pick up the kids from school. Life did proceed as normal on the outside of my little orbit. Veronica agreed to come back at 7:30 PM so we could meditate until 8:00. Then I would make the call.

By the time Veronica arrived, I was completely worn out and frazzled. I knew I had to do this, but it was the scariest thing I had ever done. She told me when she walked in my room that I almost looked gray. I was totally wiped out and could barely move. Veronica called Sandy, as we had spoken to her earlier in the day, and she agreed with our decision. I lay on my bed and listened to Veronica talk to Sandy. I told my girls what I was planning to do, and they were wonderful. They brought us candles to burn and put on soft music. Roger was still at work, but the girls waited patiently and quietly.

I picked up the phone and dialed the number. By this point, all I wanted to do was get it over with. The father answered, but I asked to speak with the mother. He asked who was calling. I didn't expect that, but I quickly replied, "Janet, from Seattle."

She got on the phone and sounded upset, but she listened patiently. I went over what I had already said in the letter. I didn't want to interfere in their lives, but I simply wanted them to know that if David wanted to know about his birth background, with their blessing, I was available.

I asked her if she had received my letter, and she replied, yes. I asked if she was doing okay, and I said that I prayed for her and her family. She said she felt in shock. She had no idea that this kind of thing could happen. They had visited a counselor about my letter and decided to wait until David graduated to tell him. She was very nervous, but then so was I.

It somehow helped to realize that we were both feeling the same emotion. We compared some notes and laughed about both our nicknames being the same. She thanked me for calling. She said she had mailed me a letter with a picture, but they had traveled out of town afterward. When she returned she found the letter still in the mailbox, as she had forgotten to put a stamp on it. She had mailed it out again with a stamp that day. She didn't appear anxious to get off the phone and kept asking me questions. We talked for ninety minutes. We seemed to get along just fine. Finally, the call was over, and I was so relieved. It turned out to be the best thing I could have done.

Veronica and I screamed when I got off the phone. The girls both cried and hugged each other and me. Veronica told me I did a great job. Roger was arriving home as we relayed the conversation to Sandy. Then I called Mom and Barb. The next morning I called my friends and family. Mary said, "Don't say a word, I'll be right down." We screamed and hashed over the whole call again and again. I was ecstatic and couldn't help spreading my joy to everyone who supported me and loved David.

Now I had to wait yet again for the letter. Julie and I traveled to the bank on Monday, and on our way home we passed our mailman. I ran to the mailbox, and amazingly it was here already. I ran as fast I ever could into the house, ripping it open as I found my chair to sit down. I looked into my son's eyes for the first time in eighteen years. It's as though I had known him my entire life. It was such a familiar face and then it hit me: *he looks like me!* Julie and I passed the picture back and forth, but I couldn't keep my eyes off that face. Julie told me that I needed to call everyone, so they could come see the picture. I just wanted to absorb it all. I had to look at him some more. The photograph was proof that I had a son—he was out there, and he looked like me.

Mary knew that I would be receiving the picture soon, so she walked in just to check if I received it yet. "He's a hunk!" she yelled and started jumping around the room. After she left, I decided I needed to call everyone. My sister Peg came by after work. She described him as gentle-looking. Later that evening, my girlfriends and I all went out for drinks. I'm sure that David would absolutely die if he could have seen us celebrating with his picture propped up in the middle of the table where we all could see it.

It took me a long time to recover from looking into that photograph. I carried it with me everywhere I went and put it on my nightstand. It was the first thing I saw in the morning as I awoke. My family and I analyzed the thing to death. He's got my eyes, my chin, your nose, and so on. In my mind, I always assumed he would look like his father. When I had last seen him as an infant, he did look like Joe. But I was so ecstatic that now he looked like me.

During the conversation with his mom, she told me they planned to wait until after his graduation to tell him—probably in July or August. I felt comfortable that they would indeed tell him as planned, and these few months gave me time to just digest all this news. I didn't have to travel to the mailbox in anticipation of news. It brought me an incredible peace. I did speak with her a few more times, and we had some very nice conversations. I always felt comfortable speaking with her.

On June 9, 1988, we got word that our CI had found Roger's birth mother. She lived about an hour away from Seattle. Rose couldn't believe that Roger found her and was very excited. She explained that the rest of her family didn't know about Roger, so she needed some time to call a family meeting and tell them. As it turned out, she had told one of her daughters earlier in life. This daughter actually shared the news with another one, so truly they were not as shocked as expected. Her only other son didn't know, however; and it was a big surprise to him. His name is also Roger, which was a bit ironic.

It took about a month before we could schedule a time to meet them. They were wonderful and accepted us right into their family. It's been great for Roger because his adoptive mom developed Alzheimer's, and his father died when he was only ten. A few of the birth family members were initially reluctant to meet Roger, but they warmed up later as they got to know him better. Rose simply asked Roger, "What took you so long?"

* * *

Our whole family spent the July Fourth weekend at the beach. I stayed with the girls while Roger drove home for work the next day. My sisters and I were standing around the campfire when my dad brought me the phone, saying, "It's Roger." I couldn't figure out why he would be calling so late. Roger quietly said, "You have a letter from Dave." I literally fell to my knees. Roger asked me if I wanted him to open it, and of course I wanted him to read it to me immediately. I was in shock, and I couldn't believe I was finally going to hear words from my son. He read it to me twice, but I finally handed the phone to Barb so that she could hear it and later tell me what it said. I was so excited that I really couldn't concentrate. All my dreams were coming true.

Dave wrote a beautiful letter. He said he had often thought about me, and he also had several friends who were adopted. They had sometimes talked about their birth parents and wondered if their birth parents thought of them the same. He said he might go to Idaho at the end of the summer and thought we could make arrangements to have him come to Seattle to meet us. He asked if that would be okay with me. I couldn't believe it, and the realization that I could meet him so soon excited me. He also included letters to the girls. By the time we hung up with Roger, I felt like I was going crazy. Adrenaline raced through my veins, and I couldn't even stand still. In the letter, David said his folks had just told him that night, and he had written his reply right away and mailed it that very same night. I called Veronica, and we screamed together.

I couldn't sleep and lay awake on the couch all night. My mother got up in the morning and just patted my head as she passed me on her way to the kitchen. Karen and I drove home first thing the next morning. I couldn't wait to see the letter and pictures Dave had sent. Roger left the letter on the kitchen table for me. I read it over and over. As soon as my sisters and friends got off work they all came over. We passed the letter and pictures around and around the table. There wasn't a dry eye in the house. One was of Dave and his prom date. They were standing in front of their fireplace and above it was the exact same picture of Jesus that Veronica had in her house. She said, "Do you know how many times I prayed to Jesus, asking him to please help us find Dave?" I was totally rummy by the end of the day and just physically and emotionally spent.

I talked to one birth mother who didn't tell anyone she was searching for her child. When she found him, she sent out birth announcements. I thought about how strong she must have been to carry the search by herself without a support network. I couldn't imagine enduring the highs and lows of the process without all the support I received. That all my sisters and friends shared this with me and that they would come to my house at a moment's notice had made the journey so incredible and comforting to me. Words cannot explain how grateful I am to all of them. The whole search process truly strengthened my bonds with so many of my friends and family.

Dave's letters to the girls were absolutely precious. You could tell he put a lot of thought into each one. By the time we had read over each letter he sent, we concluded he was the most wonderful, sensitive person. He said he hoped to meet them someday and asked them to write back and send more pictures. They couldn't wait to meet their big brother.

I replied to Dave immediately. We also started communicating by phone to try to set up arrangements for his visit. My first phone call with Dave was exciting to say the least. I told him how I was looking forward to meeting him, and he said the same. It took us a few conversations before his travel plans were set. The Idaho trip fell through, so we decided to fly him to Seattle in August. I was nervous and excited. It seemed to take a while before he replied with the actual dates and length of his trip. He would be able to stay for five days. I felt so fortunate.

Meanwhile, I wrote his folks again, thanking them for telling David about me. I reassured them that we would take good care of him and that I hoped he would return home ready for college. I explained to his parents about the beach cabin, so they knew where we would be staying. I didn't

know about the timing, but I felt it better to ease their minds knowing he would be in a beach setting rather than staying in our home in town.
I thought long and hard about the circumstances surrounding Dave's visit. Roger and I talked about it extensively. We decided that the beach house was the most comfortable and best location to get to know each other. I didn't want this to be a heavy, stressful visit for him. What a joke. How could it be anything but heavy and stressful? But the casual beach atmosphere would take the edge off somewhat.

Everyone wanted to make sure that I had enough time with Dave. I knew all my friends and family wanted to meet him. There was considerable discussion about how difficult it would be to meet my large family, let alone all my friends. The cabin provided enough space and the water provided an avenue for activities. My family would be in and out since they all had different schedules. Dave could meet them gradually as opposed to all at once. I tentatively set Sunday aside for my friends to come up for the day. I also told them that, if I thought it would be too much, then I would call them to cancel. Of course they understood. I wanted Sandy, Ron, and their boys there for at least a couple of days, but I didn't know if this would be too large of a group. Roger insisted, saying that we needed them there for Dave. Roger felt it would be ideal to have a couple of guys Dave's age to bum around with. I was delighted. I couldn't believe the thing Sandy and I dreamed about so many years ago was now going to come true. Our boys were going to be together at last—and at the beach on top of it.

Now all we had to do was wait until August. You would think that as much time as I spent waiting over the past years that I would have perfected it. We did travel to the cabin with friends, but it still seemed to take an excruciatingly long time before Dave arrived.

Finally the day was here. Thank goodness he arrived in the morning, so we just awoke early and drove to the airport. I felt every feeling possible on that morning trip. Excitement, apprehension, joy—these and other emotions pulsed through my thoughts before we arrived. We stood at the window and watched the plane slowly taxi to the gate. I cried but composed myself by the time he walked off the plane. He was almost the last one to exit. I was so afraid I would fall apart. I didn't want Dave to meet a crazy woman, so I managed to regain composure by the time he got there. I think it might have been a blessing that he was the last one. His arms were full with his bags, but I hugged him anyway and then introduced Roger and the girls. Roger took home movies. I was blessed to have Roger with his way of making people feel at ease. On the trip back from the airport, he just kept a running commentary about where we were and pointed out the highlights of the city.

While we were at the airport, my poor family and friends waited anxiously, watching the clock, talking on the phone, and guessing what was happening at every moment. They joked about going to the airport and hiding out to watch, but Roger insisted he would take the movies and that would be good enough. They could wait until a later date to meet Dave.

We brought Dave back to our home in Seattle to get packed up for the beach. He helped Roger load furniture in a truck that we needed to take up with us. We've all laughed about that one. "Hi, Dave, nice to meet you. Now help Roger load up a truck." Dave rode in the truck with Roger, and the girls rode with me in the car. I think they really started to bond, and Dave began to relax on that drive to the cabin.

The whole week couldn't have turned out better. Dave was able to meet everyone gradually as we planned. Two sisters and their husbands arrived during the first two days. I also had time to spend with Dave alone. He and I went down to the end of the beach one afternoon, and I told him about his birth and birth father—all the gory details. He was a very well-adjusted young man. He always figured his birth circumstances were what they turned out to be—a young girl getting pregnant and thinking she had no other options.

I had called and spoken to Joe's second wife, explaining that Dave was coming to town but I didn't hear a word from him. It was good for my circumstances because I didn't have to get them together. I felt good because I had given Joe every opportunity for involvement along the process. In the end, I just never heard from him. I explained to Dave that I hoped he wouldn't take it personally. Joe had always been very interested in meeting Dave, but for whatever his reasons were now, he couldn't do it.

On the next day, I really struggled with my emotions. I had asked Dave to bring some baby pictures, and he gave them to me Friday morning. I sat at the fire pit by myself and went through them, one by one. The heaviness of giving him up started to hit me on this day. What a huge mistake it had been to give him up.

Within half an hour of being at the beach on that first day, Karen and Dave were racing around, chasing each other, and getting along great. He fit in so well. It was as though he had never been lost to us. For me, after looking at the photographs, it was a day of anger, frustration, and depression. My sisters Barb and Mary Jo were very concerned about me. I felt I just needed to be alone for a while to sort through these emotions. I wanted to get back to normal and spend good times with Dave and the rest of the family. Fortunately, I managed to get through it. I took a nap and woke up feeling much better. By this time, the rest of my sisters arrived, and we sat around the kitchen table with Dave, showing him pictures of us girls when we were young.

I reexamined the whole adoption scenario in my mind. Here I was, finally with my son at my parents' beach home. My mom and dad would be arriving soon to meet Dave. Everyone was so accepting after all these years. I started to think, "Maybe if I had kept him as a baby, sooner or later they would all have come around." When I got pregnant, I thought keeping my baby meant never going home to Seattle and my family. How wrong I was. I could have come home, probably to an accepting family. But it wasn't to be. So I tried not to think about it and was so thankful that we got a second chance with this reunion. But the regret was still difficult and raw in my heart.

Sandy, Ron, and the boys arrived on their boat Saturday afternoon. I had told Dave who these people were and how they were connected to him. We watched them as the boat came in. Sandy ran up to Dave, held his face in her hands, kissed him, and said how wonderful it was to have him here finally. I can't imagine what he must have thought, with all these people making a fuss over him. He and Kelly hit it off great. They went off in the boat several times, were able to get away from the adults, and talk like boys. Kelly told me later that Dave was feeling very relaxed, much more than he thought he would be. Dave shared that he realized now how much his visit had meant to me. That night Sandy and I stood outside watching our boys in the house sit around with all the kids telling stories and laughing. Our tears flowed freely as we hugged each other.

As the five days came to an end, it was a whirlwind of goodbyes and preparations for Dave's departure. It was strange how things came out in our conversations during the five days. On our last day together, there were quite a few questions and answers. Dave asked me about the home I lived in during my pregnancy. He asked about his birth father. He wanted to know if he was as funny as Roger and Don. By the end of the week, Dave knew so much more about his birth family and the circumstances surrounding his birth.

I'm not sure the departure at the airport could have been any more depressing. We were rushed and barely had enough time to take a few pictures and say goodbye. Karen and I sobbed. We stayed until we couldn't see the plane anymore. I was so glad it was midnight, and there weren't many people around to witness all the crying and sobbing.

The next day Sandy called to say they needed to go back to the beach to get their boat, which had broken down while they were up there. I was so thankful to have this time with her to talk over the weekend. I really didn't want to be alone that day anyway. Sandy told me that Kelly said

Dave could have been a best friend. He fit in so well, and they got along as though they had known each other their whole life.

Veronica and I had many good pictures from the week. The best one was of Dave and me standing in front of a wood carved eagle, which sits next to the fire pit at the beach house. I made copies and sent them to Dave. I hoped that, when he reflected on his visit, that it would bring as many smiles to him as it did to me.

By October, I hadn't heard anything from Dave since he left. I didn't know why, and of course I thought the worst. Was he pissed, hurt, angry? Did he hate me? Then I would rationalize to myself: he's working, going to college—that he's male. I didn't want to write again. I wanted to give his mom a break. I wanted her to see that I meant what I said about not interfering in their lives. She had been gracious enough to tell him and then let him come visit.

I went to an adoption conference trying to find birth mothers who had found eighteen-year-old sons to compare behaviors. I only met a few; however, their stories didn't correlate to mine, so it really didn't help much. I ran into my counselor at the conference, and we talked quite a bit. Roger and I went to a post-reunion meeting that was excellent. Their advice was to send Thanksgiving and Christmas cards and then just wait and see what happens. I was relieved because that's what I wanted to do, and that's what I did. We all signed the holiday cards, Roger, Julie, Karen, and me. Roger wrote that Dave could call collect anytime. I sent another one to his parents, and I thanked them for being so supportive and generous. I told them I was at peace after eighteen years.

One night I had a dream. It was one of those real, vivid, true-to-life dreams. David told me that he loved me, and that everything was okay. That helped me tremendously. I didn't worry nearly as much after that. I think I realized that it might take time, but eventually everything would work out the way it should.

It didn't seem very long until it was Christmas. This was going to be a really great time for me. Year after year, I used to think about my Christmas when I was pregnant and dream of the day I would meet Michael. But this Christmas I had so much to be thankful for, and most of the hurt was gone. On Christmas night about 11:00 PM, the phone rang. I couldn't believe who would call at this time of night. Karen said it was for me.

I answered, and Dave said, "Janet, it's Dave." I must have said ten times, "I'm so glad you called."

He explained he had started to write several times but just hadn't finished. He thanked me for the pictures and told me what a good time he had. Maybe he could come back next summer? My heart skipped a beat with excitement at that question. This was the ultimate Christmas present. I didn't need to worry anymore.

Who knew what the coming years would bring. I heard the pain doesn't go away with reunions but just lessens over time. I found this to be true for me. I'll never truly have a son. I can't share those most precious moments of growing up. There are no memories of family life to share. I really had no sense of how he grew up. I know he obviously came from a loving, caring home and that he lived a happy childhood. He's a lot like me because he has many friends that he cares about deeply. I didn't know what the future held, but I knew, in my heart, that we would be in contact and build our relationship to something more significant.

The next summer we did get together again, and it seemed even better than the first time. Dave just fell back in place as though he had never left. We talked by phone numerous times throughout the year, but Dave always initiated the call. We told him he could call collect anytime. He knew how important the relationship was to me, but really he was the one who worked at developing our bond and making our relationship a priority. I didn't want to push myself into his life; instead, I waited to be invited. As we grew closer through the years and when he moved out on his own, I also felt comfortable calling him. He came to visit numerous summers, and it was always a huge family gathering.

My family and extended family love Dave, and anytime he could fit in a visit to us, everyone made it a priority to come see him. Of course the beach house was a fixture for every visit, although he did stay in our home in Seattle a few times. One particular occasion, we even included Dave and his new bride on a vacation to Hawaii. He truly became a part of our family, and I am fortunate at how my family accepted him with open arms. He was never considered a novelty to be forgotten after a brief meeting. He was a source of pride that everyone enjoyed knowing and spending time with. Several of my family members also have maintained contact with Dave throughout the year. His contact with our family was no longer strictly through me but through several individual relationships he had with others. We've managed and built a strong bond over the past twenty years now. I take great pride knowing that I have now been a part of his life for more years than the years I was absent.

Roger's Journey

I don't remember how young I was when I found out that I was adopted. It was something I knew for such a long time although I never focused on the fact. My adoptive parents never spoke about it. I think that I was just a kid whom no one wanted and was thankful my adoptive family found me. I suppose at some point during Jan's search for Dave, I began to have thoughts and questions about my own biological parents. What if they were searching for me the way that Jan searched for Dave? I witnessed my wife struggling on this emotional roller coaster while searching for her son, and I began to wonder if my own mother might struggle with these same obstacles.

Of course, once I started questioning and wondering, it just led to a stronger desire to know. I asked my adoptive mother, Gladys, about the adoption, and it really upset her. She didn't want to speak about it at all. The last thing that I desired was to upset my mom or make her feel as if her love wasn't enough for me. So I decided to put off searching for a while. When I did some research, I never let her know about it. She later developed Alzheimer's, and we had to move her to a home. During this move, Jan and I found papers in a desk from the adoption agency that really helped my case. At this point, Mom wasn't able to understand much, so we never spoke of the adoption again. My adoptive father died when I was ten years old. My mom raised me as a single mother from then on; and while we didn't have many luxuries, we had all the things we needed. She was a wonderful woman, and I was lucky to have her as a mother.

After we got the name of the adoption agency, I began to learn more about my adoption and the events leading up to it. One thing I remembered as a child was that I had a pet name for myself, Steven. Ironically, this was the name my birth mother had given me. That was a little bit of a shock. I also discovered that I had a medical condition as a baby that kept me from being adopted right away. It didn't develop into anything, but I was placed in seven different foster homes over seven months before my adoption went through. Finally, I went home with my mom and my dad.

After I found the name of my birth mother, Rose, I was really excited to meet her. She only lived forty-five minutes away, and I know I just had great expectations of establishing a relationship with her. I had heard stories of great relationships that grew from finding your family, and I just hoped we would all become one big happy family as Jan's family has been to me. I was also curious about my birth father and my heritage, so just being able to have some questions answered about myself really made me excited to meet her.

Before I went to meet Rose, I really wasn't too worried about it. I knew it would be a little awkward, but I'm a pretty easygoing guy. I'm a salesperson, so meeting new people really wasn't that intimidating to me. I know that Rose and my twin sisters were much more nervous and uncomfortable when we met. I know that she never realized the possibility that she could be found although she was happy that I searched for her. She had not ever told her family about me although her daughters somehow suspected that there had been another child. I just remember hoping that after we met, that they would like me.

At our initial meeting and others following, it became apparent that we really came from different worlds. Rose was very gracious and included our family in some of their family's activities. However, as time went on, our outlook seemed very different. I was raised in the city and had gone on to travel and find success in the business world. They lived in a very small industrial town. Rose passed away shortly after our meeting, so I was so fortunate that I found her. After her funeral, my siblings seemed like they weren't really sure how I fit into the picture. At times, it just appeared as though they weren't very interested to invite me into the family. In retrospect, I could have tried harder as well. My youngest sister and I maintain contact, and I'm hoping that will include all my siblings with time.

I think my experience made me a little more receptive and understanding of the feelings Dave might experience when he came to visit us. Of course, he was a great kid, but our entire family went to great lengths to make him feel wanted and included.

My only advice to other adoptees would be that a meeting is really worth it. I would also say that you should approach it with an open mind and heart. Just realize that it's hard for everyone. You can't have expectations that are too high in the beginning. You just need to hope that you can feel some connection, and you can build on that. Maybe it is a physical characteristic or a behavioral trait, but just anything that you can find in common and build a beginning from that connection.

Dave's Journey

I always knew that I was adopted although I'm not sure what age I was when I was told. Really the only thing that I knew about my birth mother was that I was born in Kansas City and that she was an airline stewardess. I don't remember really wondering about my birth parents or being concerned with where I came from until I was close to fifteen. I had a really good friend that I met my sophomore year of high school who was also adopted. We talked about someday finding our birth parents and just how to go about it.

My memory of when my parents told me about Janet is very clear. My senior year of high school had just ended, and I was getting ready to go out with some friends of mine. It was somewhere close to 8:00 PM, and my parents asked when I would be home because they needed to tell me something. The worst thing you can tell someone is that you "need to tell them something" because now they have to know what it is. I knew my friends were waiting in the car, but I was insistent on knowing what it could be that they felt they needed to tell me. This was when they gave me the letter from Jan.

Strangely, I didn't feel much emotion as I read the letter. For some reason, I just always felt that I would eventually find my birth parents, so it wasn't a huge shock. I now realize how naïve that was, but at the time I really didn't know any better. I recall that, after I read the letter, my parents asked if I had questions, whether I was all right, and if I was okay with all of it. I just remember not having much emotion about it at all. One of my friends waiting in the car was the one who was also adopted, so we talked about it quite a bit that night. I definitely wanted to meet Jan and the girls, but Seattle really seemed so far away. I guess it took a while for it to sink in that I would meet them shortly.

Once we made plans for my visit, I still really didn't experience any apprehension or emotion. We had spoken on the phone a few times and exchanged letters and pictures, so I felt comfortable leading up to the flight to Seattle. Previously, I had only flown one time commercially, so Seattle seemed so far away even though I knew I would see all of them in a few short hours. If you have ever flown into Seattle from east of the Cascades, then you know that one moment you are over mountains and the next you are flying over the city. It was about this time when I started to feel anxious about our meeting. I realized then I was getting ready to spend a week with a group of strangers. I recall the plane circling, and I was happy that it was buying me more time. I was in no hurry to get on the ground.

I was seated toward the back of the plane and waited until everyone left their seats before I started to grab my things. I waited as long as I could before I exited. At that point, I just really felt apprehensive about meeting Jan and her family. What if we didn't get along or just had different interests? What if they didn't like me, or what if I simply wanted to go home? I couldn't. I was stuck with them for the next week, like it or not. Once we actually met and headed to the beach house I was really surprised at how easily they included me in her family. I didn't know what to expect from all these people I would be meeting. But everyone—not just Jan, Roger, and the girls—went to great lengths to make me feel welcome. Her sisters, brothers-in-law, parents, and close friends all knew about me. I later came to understand they had celebrated my birthday, kept track of my age and grade, and constantly imagined what I might be like. They knew of me long before I knew of them. I never dreamed how close Jan was to her family and friends and how I could have been a part of their lives even though I was never around. It seemed so easy for them to show me affection whereas I was not very comfortable with it. They were more than strangers, but I hadn't known about them for very long; and I went into a relationship where they knew a lot about me.

I know that Jan gave me a lot of space, and we just allowed the relationship to grow in due time. It has been special in its unique way. She never tried to mother me, and I'm thankful my adoptive parents allowed me to continue our relationship. I'm just thankful that she worked so hard to find me.

PART TWO

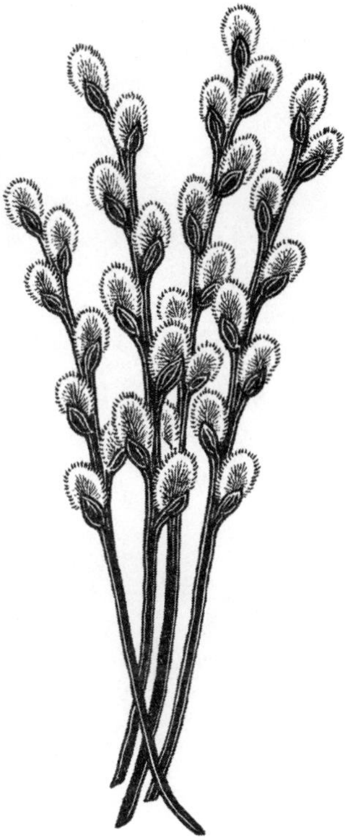

CHAPTER *one*

Reality Hits Home

A shaking finger punches in numbers on the phone—all but the very last one. She pauses and takes a deep breath. The planned conversation replays in her mind just as she rehearsed it hundreds of times throughout the day. Now, instead of pushing the last number, she hangs up and starts the rehearsal again, somehow hoping this will all go away. The tears flow silently. She doesn't want her parents to hear her torment. They can't know she's falling apart. After a few minutes, she dries her eyes, bites her lip, and picks up the phone once again.

Unplanned pregnancies make up 47 percent of all pregnancies in a given year, but in the teenage population, 87 percent of all pregnancies are not planned as reported by the American Pregnancy Association. Through the years, circumstances and options for unplanned pregnancies and unwed mothers have changed, but the emotions shared by women faced with this situation remain constant. Fear of the unknown, lack of knowledge about options, and the shame of disappointing family all create overwhelming emotions for a young girl facing an unplanned pregnancy. While statistics show the number of unplanned pregnancies has steadily declined, there are still many young women who experience this life-altering event—often with little or no support system.

Knowledge Is Power

Young girls growing up in today's society are continually bombarded with information about sex. They see sexual images in every form of media, followed by contraceptives openly advertised in regular television programming, magazines, and on the Internet. Compared with teenagers of only twenty years ago, today's young women prove to be extremely knowledgeable about the physical mechanics and consequences of sexual behavior. In fact, they are fed information at younger and younger ages. Elementary schools now have extensive programs geared to empower young girls with knowledge about their bodies and what to expect as they develop into women.

Many women recall that generations of women in the past may have learned about sex from a friend during a talk in a locker room or from a black and white diagram of the female reproductive system in health class. If a mother did talk to her daughter about sex, it was predominantly about the physical mechanics of a sperm fertilizing an egg. But what about the psychological and emotional implications of sex? Unfortunately, these were often left for a girl to "figure out" by herself or to learn from older friends. The very thought of talking about sex seemed "dirty," and girls with good reputations would never even let those thoughts enter their mind, much less have a conversation about it.

In the last few decades, it has also become easier to obtain contraceptives, even at a young age. Title X of the Public Health Service Act was established in 1970 to provide family planning services to women regardless of their economic status. It was meant to offer assistance to women in family planning with contraceptives and medical care. Unlike Medicaid, which offers assistance after a pregnancy has been confirmed,

Title X helps many women prevent the pregnancy in the first place. Title X seeks to decrease the possibility of abortion and the ramifications of single motherhood by offering preventive measures instead of reactive solutions after a pregnancy has already occurred.

The results of Title X have so far been favorable. The Guttmacher Institute reports that from 1988 to 2008 the teenage pregnancy rate has dropped 28 percent, with rates dropping in all fifty states as well as Washington DC. This reduction also has resulted in a reduction in abortions by 50 percent. The diminishing trend can be attributed to more young women remaining abstinent and the more prevalent use of contraceptives. However, in a recent study, according to the Centers for Disease Control and Prevention, in 2005–2006, teen pregnancy rates increased by 3 percent, which was the first increase in over fourteen years. Also, childbearing by unmarried women rose 20 percent from 2002 to 2006. These are not alarming increases since there has been a steady decline over time, but the fact that there is any increase concerns health professionals nonetheless. Every single unplanned pregnancy has tremendous implications in many lives and is not merely a number; rather, it's a woman with a story and intense financial and emotional issues to face.

Statistics are easy to read without feeling the emotion involved. But even though rates have decreased over time, there are still many fearful girls faced with the consequences of sexual behavior. Knowledge is a powerful tool, but we must look at our society and certain views that send mixed messages to today's young women and help them understand the long-term emotional consequences of sexual activity.

The Invincibility of Youth

We know that simply being young gives a certain sense of invincibility. The excitement of new experiences and the increased freedom that comes with the teen years play into this false sense of security. While there are those who would never question the argument that seat belts should be worn as a safety precaution, there is still intense debate surrounding the availability of contraceptives for teens. The logic that providing the means for safe sex promotes promiscuity is like saying that wearing a seat belt promotes reckless driving. Yet, the debate still rages on.

Even with the availability of tremendous informational resources, many youths still believe many sexual falsehoods such as "I can't get pregnant the first time," "My boyfriend pulls out, so we're safe," or "I just had my period, so I won't get pregnant." The world is full of these misconceptions, but the truth is the only foolproof way of not getting pregnant is to not have sex. Just like the only foolproof way not to be in a car accident is not to drive. A seat belt is not invincible and cannot guarantee that you won't get hurt in an accident; it only increases the probability that you will survive. Likewise, good contraceptive practices do not guarantee you will not get pregnant, but it does decrease your chances of a pregnancy. Of sexually active teens who did not use contraceptives, 90 percent became pregnant in the first year. Denying the probability does not change the facts.

Another rampant belief among those practicing unprotected sex is that it offers a sense of excitement and spontaneity. To some, they believe the experience is heightened with this sort of "danger." Certainly, it is a personal preference; but no matter how the experience rates, it still has permanent consequences. It is also not uncommon for teen girls to fantasize that their partner will take care of them if they had a baby, romanticizing pregnancy as a way to get their partner to love them more. While the rare instance does exist that this romantic ending works out for the young woman, the majority of teenage pregnancies leave her without any support from her partner. Laws help gain financial support from the father, but so many times the young woman is left emotionally abandoned and must still face hard decisions about her life and her pregnancy.

Another flawed thought process involves the idea that getting pregnant is acceptable if one is not prepared for sex. They think if it "just happened"—or better yet, they were impaired by drugs or alcohol—then the accountability is somehow lessened. In the end, they still will be the ones to reap the consequences, no matter whose fault it was, what condition they were in, or how it happened. The same child is conceived, and the same problems arise from an unplanned pregnancy. The circumstances make no difference in the end result.

Our Conflicting Society

We live in a world heavily influenced by images from the media, and they surround us no matter where we are. Teenagers today are pushed toward abstinence programs in school and churches, but on TV, movies, radio, and the Internet, sex is the predominant theme. Most of what they see involves hype about how fun sex is, the joy of "love," and how to be seductive and attractive—all of which conflict with the message of abstinence. While abstinence is the only true safety net from an unplanned pregnancy, there is still so much taboo surrounding sex that open and honest communication on the subject can be hard to find. Teens receive conflicting messages from adults, teachers, lawmakers, and the media.

Religious beliefs of the family can also be a stumbling block in communication. Certainly, it may help a young person remain sexually inactive; but once they choose to engage in sex, religion can limit the teen's openness with the family or others who might be able to provide good and helpful information. Many teen girls think that they can no longer be viewed as a "good" girl if they are sexually active. Hence, these young women tend to avoid contraception because it is viewed as more "immoral" if you plan to have sex. It's much easier to justify if it just "happened" or if it were an accident. Often the embarrassment of purchasing contraceptives or the fear of their parents' finding out about an exam will keep a teen from doing anything at all. They often view the taking of contraceptives as though they are planning to sin.

Young women in this predicament live with shame, fear, and denial in hopes that pregnancy won't happen to them. Consequently, they may feel a more negative response from their family if they do become pregnant. This negative response is due to the fact that they not only feel shame themselves, but that they have brought shame upon their family as well. It feels as if the outside world is pushing for sex; but once the act has been performed, there are negative consequences for that behavior. For example, society will negatively label young women who engage in sex. Young people are sent mixed signals about certain behaviors. They are told to tolerate all kinds of behaviors and later are subjected to condemnation because they suffered the consequences of one of those "tolerated" behaviors.

Once a pregnancy is confirmed, the most important step is to find a way to deal with the news emotionally. Denial is not a solution, but many young women will wait for months, hoping that the pregnancy will disappear or that they will "think of something" to fix the problem. Some even continue destructive behaviors, such as drinking and smoking, because they cannot bring themselves to face the imminent responsibility of a child. They don't realize that the responsibility began at conception and that they can greatly impact the development of the child with these abusive behaviors. For this reason, it is important to accept the news and immediately begin planning for their future.

It is of the utmost importance for the young woman to make herself and her health, physical and emotional, a priority. Doctors or counselors can offer many options and solutions to help young women stay as healthy as possible. Many young women also benefit from a support group where they can visit with other young women experiencing the same physical and emotional issues. Simply knowing that one is not alone does much to improve anyone's outlook and hope for the future.

Keeping a journal often has a positive impact on young pregnant women in that it provides a place for them to allow their emotions to have an outlet. It is normal for anyone who is pregnant to experience a multitude of emotions in any given day. However, it is not healthy to suppress these emotions or keep them inside. It is important for people to have a release for their emotions somewhere, whether by writing, contributing in a support group, or simply talking to a close friend. These options will allow one to get clear of the emotional baggage and prepare to make some critical decisions about the future of the pregnancy.

CHAPTER SUMMARY

- Sex is constantly being pushed on young women in today's society, but consequences are rarely portrayed.
- Planning for sex or using birth control sometimes makes girls from strict religious backgrounds feel wrong. Instead, they frequently opt for no protection.
- Some girls falsely believe that if they get pregnant, their boyfriend will automatically take care of them and their baby.
- Physical health of the mother and baby is critical from the time of conception.
- Emotional health of the mother is very important, and she needs to establish a support system for a better pregnancy experience.

QUESTIONS

1.

2.

3.

4.

5.

6.

7.

8.

9.

10.

CHAPTER two

Decisions, Decisions

After the initial shock a woman experiences when she learns that she is pregnant, it is important to tell those who will be affected the most by the information. This includes the baby's father and the young woman's parents. It is not uncommon for a person to share the information with a close and trusted friend first to gain support for what is to come. Talking through the emotions associated with the shock can help a woman face the difficult emotional traumas she must endure to make good decisions.

Verbalizing information and options to another person helps release the emotions and bring a calmer demeanor when she must tell the father and other family members. Later, these close, supportive friends provide great support, as needed, once the information is shared with others. If a close friend is not available or an option, then seeking a counselor to discuss the situation can meet the same need. Many organizations help young women with unplanned pregnancies, and they employ support counselors to help people come to terms with the emotions of the situation and to provide a foundation on which to build.

In the best situation, the father plans to be involved with the birth and care of the new baby. If he wants to offer support, then consideration should also be given to his opinion on what options to take with the pregnancy. The news that he is the father can be an emotional shock to any young man, and often they don't react with tactfully or with some level of thoughtfulness. They tend to react emotionally just as the young woman does, and this tendency should be taken into consideration if his first reaction isn't very positive. Some items to consider when thinking about talking to the prospective father include the following:

- Confirm the pregnancy with a pregnancy test so there is no speculation about the situation. Be prepared for an initial reaction of disbelief, or the question, "Is it mine?" Answer his questions honestly, and remember that the first reaction is usually pure emotion and doesn't necessarily reflect on the relationship.
- Choose a time and place when both parties are relaxed and in a good mood. Telling someone about something of this magnitude during an argument isn't fair to either person, as the reactions tend to be even more emotional and are often hurtful.
- Make sure that there is enough time to discuss the situation fully and to answer his questions. One should not expect things to go well if the explanation is rushed or if there are distractions to the conversation.
- Be positive. Do not set up the conversation by saying that there is some horrible news. If he picks up a positive attitude about the situation, he is more likely to react in a positive manner.
- Be prepared for many different reactions and emotions. He may be angry, scared, or sad; he may also experience a multitude of emotions all at once. Remember that everyone should be allowed time to deal with their emotions. He may be silent simply because he doesn't know the right thing to say. Most importantly, remember that

many young men react in a certain way to the initial news but act differently after they have had some time to rethink the situation.

If the father is absent, as in many cases, the young woman should seek help from family and close friends. Telling her parents is probably the most difficult hurdle for the young woman. While there will be an initial shock and, possibly anger, remember that most parents eventually soften their hearts as their acceptance of the reality grows. Suggestions for telling parents differ as well, but the critical issue is that they are told before they hear it from someone else. Some suggestions follow:

- Writing a letter is often a good way to communicate the news with parents, especially if the young woman is fearful of their initial reaction. In a letter, most people are better able to communicate their emotions without fear of interruption. A letter also gives parents time to process the news and gain control of their emotions before they react openly.
- Sometimes having a close personal friend or family member to offer support helps both sides. A trusted aunt or pastor can give stability to the situation and help keep emotions at a reasonable level.
- It is important for the woman to wait a short time after initially finding out that she is pregnant so that she is more able to adjust and communicate in a calm manner. The more emotional the teller is, the more emotional the reactions of others will likely be. Once the parents see the young woman as calm, then they realize that they will be okay. In most cases, their daughter's well-being is their primary concern.
- Be prepared for reactions of shock, disbelief, anger, silence, and sadness. Once again, realize that first reactions and later thoughts about the pregnancy often differ considerably. Be willing to allow time for them to comprehend the situation.

If there is serious concern about a violent or abusive reaction, then contact a crisis pregnancy center or safe haven. They always offer support counselors and resources to keep individuals in this situation safe. At this point, the mother's health and safety must be the main priority. It is imperative that the young woman find someone to support her so that she does not face the unknowns of pregnancy alone.

Once the pregnancy is established and the people who are directly affected are notified, it is important to choose a doctor or clinic to provide care during the pregnancy. Sometimes this choice depends on insurance or lack thereof, financial status, and the path chosen for the pregnancy. If the parents and/or the baby's father offer support, then they may help in the decision of the care provider.

Unplanned pregnancy centers are a wonderful resource for information on doctors and financial assistance. They can also offer information on the three options for your pregnancy: (1) keeping your baby, (2) giving your baby up for adoption, and (3) having an abortion. This decision is certainly not an easy one to contemplate and should not be made hastily. It is wise to involve all the individuals in the support system in this decision if it is possible. Ultimately, the choice affects the mother the greatest. It is also critical that she understand all the implications and does not make the decision based on the opinion of another. All three choices result in distinct lifelong emotional consequences, so it is imperative that the mother believes her choice is the best one for herself.

There are several issues the mother should consider when weighing one option against the others. Answering the following questions will likely help clarify the option best suited for her and her situation. Again, it may be helpful to keep a journal to write questions, answers, and thoughts during this time to reflect the decision is contemplated. It is an excellent method for keeping random thoughts and concerns throughout the day and reducing the feeling of being overwhelmed by the magnitude of the decision. For the prospective mother, here are some questions that can help you decide the best course of action for yourself:

- Do you have support of the baby's father, your parents, or other family members? Is there someone willing to offer financial and emotional support, or are you going to go through the experience alone?
- Will you be able to continue school or your job during this time? Do you have anyone to care for you if you get sick or require bed rest?
- Do you have the financial resources to pay for a doctor and hospital expenses?
- Do you have a job or the financial support to care for the baby after the birth?
- If you are attending school, will you have to drop out after the birth, or do you have support from someone so that you can continue your education?
- What religious beliefs do you have that influence this decision?
- How much is the baby's father planning to support and be involved?
- What does your family think is the best decision?

The Choice of Abortion

All states allow abortions, but most have restrictions. Individual states mandate how abortions can be performed and may require one or more of the following:

- Parental notification and/or consent
- A waiting period between zero and seventy-two hours
- Mandatory counseling

Please check with your state to receive the most updated information.

COMPLICATIONS

Physical complications of an abortion include blood loss and infection. In rare cases, there can be damage to the uterine wall, the cervix, or even the bowels. All reputable doctors will counsel patients of these possible complications, along with giving information on procedures to take if the patient experiences complications. No medical procedure is entirely foolproof, including childbirth, so it is important to understand the nature of the procedure and the possible side effects or long-term effects.

The emotional consequences remain a significant area of controversy among many, particularly since abortion itself is such a controversial and moral subject. Look in any bookstore or search online, and you will find advocates of pro-choice and pro-life with documented convincing arguments on both sides. To make the best decision possible for your situation, it is imperative to look at both sides of the situation. So many times when faced with a crisis, you may look only at the present or the immediate future. With an unplanned pregnancy, it is also important to focus on long-term effects for years to come and to include this knowledge as you make your decision. Some women will experience the emotional toll of an abortion for many years. It is wise to include the opinions of trusted individuals, but the decision will be yours to live with. So, realize that you must make it and live with it in the end. Most health professionals will also counsel you prior to an abortion to determine if you are being pressured against your will.

The Choice of Adoption

Adoption is the process of birth parents transferring their legal rights to allow adoptive parents to raise a child. Laws vary from state to state, but in recent years, there has been a movement to give birth mothers more flexibility in the choice of adoptive parents and a larger degree of involvement in the child's life. Important strides to adoption procedures and law have been made in the last twenty-five years to give birth mothers more rights and to allow for the possibility of having a relationship with the child. The next chapter is about adoption and the available options.

The Choice to Parent

The ability to parent is often considered one of the most challenging and rewarding undertakings a person can experience. The realization that life truly is a gift to be cherished and the privilege to watch a young child grow into a unique individual with a personality, interests, and traits create a sense of awe for the miracle of life. Being a parent, however, requires considerable resources in time, personal energy, and finances. Rewarding as it is, the difficulties and strains of parenting are many. For this reason, it is important to have an understanding of all your child's needs. When a young woman is considering the possibility of raising a child, she must consider the following questions:

- If you are not married, will the father of the child be able to offer support, either emotionally or financially? Is marriage a possibility, or what does the future relationship with him look like?
- Do you have any family to help (e.g., with living accommodations, childcare, finances)?
- What do you need to live on your own with the baby?
- Could you continue to reach your goals and better your own life and your child's?
- Would federal assistance programs, like WIC or Medicaid, be an option for you?
- Have you spoken with a pregnancy counselor or pastor to discuss your ability to be a good parent?

- Are you prepared emotionally to put the needs and wants of your child above your own?
- How do your religious or moral views affect your idea of the role of parent?

Some women who have a strong family support system opt to let a family member keep the child for a while until the mother is in a better position to care for it. These instances may occur if the mother needs to finish school or work for a while to earn money to move out on her own. Of course in this situation, you must have a tremendous amount of trust in the person you choose to care for your child. This is another option that could reunite you with your child later if your present situation does not allow you the freedom to be a good parent.

The key to making the best choice for your situation is researching as much information as possible and evaluating your circumstances in light of that information. Opinions are great, but you must take responsibility for doing your own research and ultimately choosing the best option for you and your child. The Internet offers a wealth of information on all aspects of pregnancy. Having a clear understanding of your options will help relieve some fears of the unknown future.

CHAPTER SUMMARY

- Young women should allow some time to fully gain control of their emotions before telling the father and parents about the pregnancy.
- It is a good idea to have a trusted friend or family member go as support, especially if the mother is fearful of the reaction.
- Having a support system of friends and family for the birth mother will help in choosing the right option for her circumstances.
- All choices—keeping the baby, adoption, and abortion—have lifelong consequences.
- To make the best choice for the situation, it is important to gather all available information so that the choice does not rely strictly on emotions but factual evidence as well.

QUESTIONS

1.

2.

3.

4.

5.

6.

7.

8.

9.

10.

CHAPTER three

Adoption

Adoption involves a court action wherein a parent relinquishes his or her parental rights to a child and the court grants those rights to adoptive parent(s). Adoption allows birth parent(s) to place the child permanently within a new family, along with transferring all rights concerning the raising of the child. The adopted child becomes a legal member of the new family once the process is finalized. However, it is not a sign of failure or admittance that the birth mother would be a bad parent. Adoption is a great sign of love for allowing the child to be raised in more positive circumstances. Many people misjudge the motivation of a woman placing her child up for adoption. The reasons are many, but ultimately the birth mother is choosing the needs of her child as her top priority.

Adoptions have decreased steadily since the 1970s. In 1940, there were 50,000 adoptions in the U.S.; in 1970, the year with the greatest number of adoptions, there were 175,000 recorded. Rates steadily decreased with the improvement of birth control and the passage of Roe vs. Wade to legalize abortion. However, in 1997, the Adoption Institute's Public Opinion Benchmark survey found that 58 percent of all Americans have been affected by adoption by either knowing an adopted child, parents who adopted, or a birth parent who relinquished his or her rights to the child. In the United States, 2 percent of all children are adopted. For a woman facing an unplanned pregnancy, adoption offers a loving option to provide for the child in way the birth mother is not prepared to do.

Birth Father

Many times in the process of adoption, the birth father is given little consideration. In fact, a birth mother cannot be forced by the legal system or a social worker to name the father unless she is willing. If she withholds the information or cannot name the father, then it is so documented. Adoptive parents often refuse to work with someone who declines to name the father. Most legal experts agree that it is extremely important to involve the birth father if at all possible. There have been several highly publicized cases where children were given up for adoption without the birth fathers' consent. They later regained custody after much heartache and considerable legal costs and fees. The emotional toll put tremendous stress on the birth fathers and the adoptive parents.

It is widely accepted that a birth mother experiences a deep sense of sadness when she gives her baby up, but the father's anguish has been largely ignored until recent years. However, in many adoptions, the father chooses to stay absent. In years past, the birth mother and legal officials were often satisfied with the birth father's absence because it facilitated the adoption process. In later years, this assumption created obstacles as birth fathers' rights began to be recognized; efforts to include the birth father in the adoption process continue to improve.

In many cases, the birth father feels pushed out of the decision-making process, which creates resentment and can later result in legal issues with the adoption. Attorneys usually find it easier to deal with the birth father early in the proceeding, including them in the process and making sure their rights are also honored. Just as a birth mother wants what is best for her baby, the father generally wants the same. Sometimes the emotional state of their relationship clouds the judgment about what is in the child's best interests. In recent years, there have been support groups for birth fathers as well as birth mothers. Research concludes that the birth father often feels an incredible sadness and considerable guilt similar to that of the birth mother. These emotions can later affect their future relationships and marriages. It is critical for these men to feel support for their loss as well. So many times in adoption cases, the birth father is simply assumed not to care about the child. In recent years, a slow movement has grown to incorporate more male social workers to deal with birth fathers, their emotions, and their rights with respect to the adoption process. Most often, the birth father's ultimate concern is the welfare of the child; when he is treated as a part of the solution, he typically will work to create a plan that best fits the needs of the child and birth mother.

Naming the birth father is also an important point if the adopted child ever needs or wants to contact his or her birth parents. Family medical issues and history can also be critical for an adopted child to know. Many adopted children eventually search for their birth parents simply to answer the call of curiosity; some search for their birth parents for genealogy. By not naming the birth father, the birth mother creates a dead end for the adopted child's personal history and search for relatives.

Private Adoption

When a private agency is chosen to handle an adoption, the birth parents give their parental rights to the agency, and then at a later date, the agency transfers the child to the adoptive parents. Although the birth parents are usually involved in choosing the adoptive family, the agency acts as the intermediary. The agency is an advocate for both parties. Its representatives see that the birth mother is treated well during her pregnancy and after the birth. They also work to represent prospective parents who are looking to adopt and then find a match to benefit both parties. Most agencies also offer counseling services to both sets of parents before and after the adoption.

Many women choose to go to a maternity home to await the birth of their child once they have decided to place the baby up for adoption. These homes typically handle the medical needs of the woman and provide a healthy, safe place to live until the arrival of the child. The agency also matches prospective adoptive parents' files to criteria set by the birth mother but also allows her freedom in choosing her baby's future family. Legal counsel is also provided; and while the birth mother receives no compensation for the child, all legal and medical expenses are covered. Maternity homes have decreased over the years with the decline in unwanted pregnancies and the increase in private adoptions. In the late 1960s, there may have been as many as three hundred maternity homes in the United States, with some serving many women. However, by the early 1980s, the Interagency Task Force on Adoption's report, "America's Waiting Children," states that there were only one hundred maternity homes left nationwide. There are often waiting lists to get into a home, so it is important to decide early on in the pregnancy if this is an option that may benefit you.

There are also agencies that handle the adoption process independently from a maternity home. Every state allows licensed private agencies to place children with adoptive parents. These agencies may charge fees to provide counseling services to the birth parents, do background checks, match potential adoptive parents, keep records of the child's medical and social history, and direct the final adoption placement. Some agencies are supported by religious organizations while others remain independent from any church sponsorship. These agencies also offer support groups and resources for counseling to both the adoptive and birth parents.

Independent Adoption

Independent adoption occurs when the birth parents relinquish their parental rights directly to the adoptive parents through an adoption attorney. State laws vary on their regulations of independent adoptions, but they are not authorized in Colorado, Connecticut, Delaware, and Massachusetts. The remaining states allow an adoption intermediary that is not a licensed child placement agency to assist birth parents in finding an adoptive family, or vice versa. These intermediaries are typically adoption attorneys knowledgeable in state regulations where the adoption is finalized. The attorney plays a vital role in the process, as they must be aware of the specific adoption laws that apply in the given state.

One major difference between agency adoption and independent adoption is that adoptive parents can "advertise" for a satisfactory birth mother. The adoptive parents and their attorney play an active role in the search for a match with a birth mother. They may use advertisements, the Internet, and networking through friends and family. Thirty-four states currently allow advertisements. However, the screening process of adoptive families is not regulated in independent adoptions as it is in state-regulated agencies. For this reason, it is important that the birth parents retain an intermediary to represent their concerns.

The adoption attorney will also be responsible for making sure the birth father consents to the adoption and that all legalities for the particular state are addressed. Typically, the adoptive parents are the ones who hire the attorney and actively search for a birth mother. However, it is a wise legal practice to have an attorney for both sides at the time of the actual adoption and transfer of parental rights. In this instance, both birth and adoptive parents feel secure in having their needs and rights established and met legally. For the birth parents, it is important to have separate legal counsel so that their interests are met by someone not working for the adoptive parents. There is greater flexibility offered in adoptions through this method, including allowing the birth parents to be a part of the child's life. The extent the birth parents remain in the child's development needs to be stated explicitly in the legal process so that neither side is misinformed of the other's intentions. Great initial communication prevents many disagreements or misunderstandings at a future date. Some adoption experts caution birth parents against independent adoptions because they may undertake a risk by not having legal representation (i.e., an economic risk). As long as the birth parents retain a reputable adoption expert to represent their interests, the independent adoption can go as smoothly as an agency adoption.

Most states' laws allow the adoptive parents to pay living, medical, and legal expenses for the birth mother. Nearly all states prohibit payment to the intermediaries for finding children although sometimes the adoptive parents can be charged reasonable service fees if approved by the court. No states allow the exchange of money for a child (with the exception of the aforementioned expenses).

Some adoptive parents choose independent adoption because they might not meet the screening criteria required by the agencies. These prospective adoptive parents might be too old or too young or have had previous marriages, health issues, other children, or a sexual orientation deemed undesirable by state law. Independent adoptions also give the adoptive parents more control over matching with the birth mother. There are significant expenses for advertising, travel to screen prospective birth mothers, and medical and legal expenses. Independent adoptions can also be time consuming before a willing birth mother is found. The National Adoption Information Clearinghouse (NAIC) estimates a private agency adoption costs the adoptive parents between $4,000 and $30,000 and that independent adoptions range between $8,000 and $30,000.

Closed Adoptions

Closed adoptions are becoming less prevalent in today's typical adoption process. It refers to the adoption in which there is no interaction or exchange of identifying information between the birth and adoptive parents. Non -identifying information, such as medical history and physical characteristics, may be shared between both parents. State legalities also play a role in the information allowed for a closed adoption.

Although every adoption has individual circumstances, closed adoptions do offer some advantages to all parties; some of those advantages are bulleted as follows.

- Fear—Birth mothers often worry about how they would answer questions concerning their pregnancy and the reason for placing a child up for adoption. Knowing that records are closed allows them to feel a sense of security against future judgment.
- Privacy—Some individuals are extremely private. A closed adoption offers a sense of security to personal privacy to both birth mothers and adoptive parents.
- Closure—Some adoptive parents and birth mothers appreciate a sense of closure after the adoption that allows them to move on in their lives. The severing of ties provides a clear end, which sometimes allows for a cleaner new start.
- Clear parental roles/boundaries—Adoptive parents feel a greater sense of security because there is no interference or interaction from birth parents.
- Time freedom—The adoptive family does not have to "share" the child with visitations, holidays, or special milestones.
- Undesirable birth parents/circumstances—A closed adoption can protect the child from learning of undesirable aspects of their birth or birth parent such as rape, drug abuse, or abandonment.

The important aspect of a closed adoption is that all parties are in agreement. However, it is also important for all parties to realize that even when an adoption is closed, records can be opened at a later date depending on state laws and the desire of the child.

Closed adoptions have lost popularity in the last twenty years. Closed adoptions might have one or more of the following unintended negative effects, which has caused its less frequent use:

- Guilt—The birth parents may feel a greater sense of guilt if they cannot share concern with their child. They may believe their child will feel abandoned.
- Grief—With any adoption, there is a period of grief for the birth parent; however, when all means of communication is removed, they often feel a greater sense of loss and experience a longer grieving period.
- Fear—Adoptive parents may feel an increased fear of the birth parents returning to want their child back. Since there is no communication to alleviate these fears, the adoptive parents constantly feel this return lurking at all times.
- Medical information—Even though medical information is provided at birth—if a medical crisis develops—the possibility of obtaining a more thorough and helpful history remains nearly impossible.
- Depression—An inability to know the well-being of their child often increases the chances the birth parents will experience long-term depression.
- Questions—An adopted child may become preoccupied with identity questions about their birth and subsequent adoption. These unresolved answers can often cause developmental problems or fears.
- Lack of information—An adopted child may have many questions concerning genealogy, family characteristics, strengths, and traits that go unanswered when records are sealed. They often feel a loss of family or simply that something is "missing."

- Confusion—Adoptive parents worry the child will be confused about who the real parents are and also worry about interference from the birth parents.

Open Adoptions

The trend in the past twenty years is to allow more communication between birth parents and prospective adoptive families. Agencies encourage the involvement of the birth parents in choosing the adoptive parents for their child. This communication is viewed as healthy for all involved. The amount of contact varies depending on the circumstances, the individual parents, and the legal agreement between the parties. Some of the positive advantages of an adoption include the following:

- Control—Birth parents often feel a much greater sense of security and control when they are involved in the process of choosing the adoptive parents.
- Fear—Birth mothers often feel less uncertainty and fear about the future well-being of their child when they play a vital role in the choice of their future family.
- Less grief—Birth parents always mourn for their loss, but the ability to maintain communication with the adoptive parents and child helps alleviate and lessen the sense of grief.
- Relationships—Developing a relationship with both the child and the adoptive family creates a sense of bonding that is healthy for all individuals involved.
- Unfounded fears—Adoptive parents feel a greater sense of security with an open line of communication with the birth parents. Typically a cooperative relationship develops rather than one that tends to be adversarial.

- Medical/family history—Even though medical history is transferred at the initial adoption proceeding, other problems may develop in either the child's or the birth parents' lives. The birth parent may find a certain disease or disorder runs in the family, or the child may need to know certain family history for a particular treatment.
- Security—Adoptive parents feel a larger sense of security knowing that the birth parents chose them out of all prospective parents.
- Identity—The adopted child feels a greater sense of identity and heritage. Irrational fear of abandonment is often eliminated when they learn the circumstances of their birth and their birth parents.
- Support—The adopted child has a larger network of people who love and support him or her. No one can ever feel too much love from too many individuals.

Opinions differ between people and circumstances. Even though open adoptions have gained in popularity, there still are disadvantages associated with this process. A few of the shortcomings of open adoptions are as follows:

- Relationship boundaries—Both the adoptive and birth parents must establish healthy boundaries in the developing relationship. Communication and honesty are critical for both parties to feel security.
- Trust—As with any close relationship, trust can be abused by either party. Strong emotions emerge when a child is involved; and if one of the parents betrays a trust in the original agreement, then the relationship is severely damaged.
- Change of heart—The adoptive parents can decide not to honor the open communication at any time. If this happens, the birth parents and adopted child may feel a huge sense of rejection.

- Unstable families—The child and adoptive family may experience disappointment and confusion if the birth parents act irresponsibly or have unstable behaviors.
- Added responsibility—The adoptive parents may feel an unhealthy responsibility for emotional responsibility to the birth parents.
- Rejection—If a situation develops where communication is stopped, then the child may feel a greater sense of rejection and abandonment.
- Struggle with control—An adopted teenager may try to manipulate parents against each other to gain control in a situation.
- Guilt—Adopted children may feel guilt about feelings and emotions associated with the different parents. They may feel they are betraying their adoptive parents for developing a relationship with the birth parents.

Each family must decide which options are important and critical to the success of their adoption. While no process is always perfect or infallible, it is wise to weigh the options to decide the best avenue for your family.

Semi-Open Adoption

Much as it sounds, the semi-open adoption is a combination of the open and closed adoption processes. The birth parents are typically involved in the selection process of the adoptive family. Records are readily shared; however, there is no physical meeting and identifying information is not released. A third party, usually an adoption agency, is responsible for the transfer of information. Communication may continue to be exchanged between the parents, but typically in the form of emails, cards, or letters. The child can gain information from the adoption professional, but he or she does not have physical contact or a direct line of communication with the birth parent. Privacy is maintained for both sets of parents, but information is readily shared as it is needed or requested.

CHAPTER SUMMARY

- Birth fathers have rights in the adoption process.
- Private adoption involves an agency. The child is first relinquished to the agency, and parental rights are later transferred to the adoptive parents.
- Independent adoption is when the birth parents relinquish their rights directly to the adoptive parents.
- Closed adoption is when all records are sealed, and there is no identifying information given to either the adoptive or birth parents.
- Open adoptions are more common in the present day. Typically the birth parents are allowed some visitations, as well as periodic updates on the child. Information is readily exchanged between the two sets of parents.
- Semi-open adoptions use an intermediary, such as the adoption agency, to transfer information. There are no visitation arrangements, but health questions and updates are handled through the intermediary.

QUESTIONS

1.

2.

3.

4.

5.

6.

7.

8.

9.

10.

CHAPTER *four*

Life Goes on—What to Expect after Adoption

In the majority of adoption cases, the birth mother decides before the actual birth if she will place the baby up for adoption. She most often makes arrangements with an agency or with an adoptive family through an attorney. However, adoptions cannot legally be performed until after the birth of the child. The final decision must be made again by the birth mother, and she remains free to change her mind even though previous verbal agreements may be in place.

States vary considerably on length of time between the birth and when the child can be legally placed for adoption. Some states allow for "intent to relinquish" papers to be signed prior to the birth, but even these can be reversed if the birth mother changes her mind. During this time, an adoption counselor verifies that the birth mother is not being coerced or forced to give up her child against her will. In some states, the legal description of the relinquishment is called "Voluntary Termination of Parental Rights." It is illegal for the birth mother to be coerced into entering the relinquishment process if she is placed under pressure by her family, the adoption agency, lawyers, or the prospective adoptive parents. There is no state law that obligates an expectant mother to relinquish her child because she accepted financial or other assistance from future adoptive parents or an agency. Idaho is the only state that requires the expectant mother to reimburse the adoptive parents or agency for services or aid given if she later revokes a signed consent for relinquishment.

For the birth mother, it is normal to experience many doubts and mixed emotions after the birth of her child. Birth is one of the most traumatic experiences a woman's body can endure, and afterward, hormones fluctuate continuously for weeks. It is an emotional time even under the best of circumstances. At this time, it is, of course, prudent for the birth mother to rethink the adoption decision and revisit the process to be sure the correct decision has been made, but it is also wise to remember the reasons for placing the baby up for adoption. If she trusted the wisdom of family and friends, then at this point she needs to ask them for support in the decision to follow through.

Sometimes it is hard for a young woman to reach out or ask others for support. The people closest to her often mistakenly think she handles the situation and truly doesn't need anyone. It is critical for family and friends of a young woman involved in an adoption to offer love and support even if she doesn't actively seek it out. Adoption is a difficult process, and she needs a support system. Birth mothers should expect an onslaught of doubt and conflicting emotions during this time, but with support, they do not have to be ruled by them.

Once the birth mother decides to continue with the adoption, there are several scenarios that can occur. Some are dictated by the adoption laws of the state, and others are governed by the type of adoption (open or closed) and the motivation of both the birth mother and adoptive parents. The actual relinquishment may take place in a court or may be signed at the agency or in front of designated officials. Some states terminate parental rights upon the relinquishment, while others consider this only a portion of a lengthy legal process. Most of these laws detail whether there is a period of time where the relinquishing parent can revoke her consent. In some areas, relinquishment is irrevocable, and in other areas, there is a probationary period. The most critical component is retaining a competent adoption lawyer familiar with all the governing laws in the state where the adoption takes place.

In the case of a closed adoption, the mother often signs the relinquishment papers before she leaves the hospital. She can only see the baby a few times, if at all, after the birth. The adoptive parents may also receive the baby at the hospital. In other instances, the mother may have a few days, or even weeks with her baby before the actual relinquishment occurs. If it is a closed adoption, then the two sets of parents will never see each other and the actual transfer of the child is assisted by an intermediary, usually the agency.

With the growing popularity of open adoptions, the process of transferring the child has become a more significant ritual. Some parents actually celebrate the transfer with both sets of parents and families present. This not only allows the birth parents to be a part of the joy celebrated by the adoptive parents, but it also begins a bond that often later results in a stronger relationship between the two sets of parents. Birth parents often choose to videotape the ceremony as a remembrance of their special time with their child. In all cases, the birth parents must be given time to say goodbye to their child. Whether it is alone quietly or with many others during an official ceremony, the birth parents need the closure of an actual goodbye and transfer to the new family.

Another popular practice is for the birth parents to keep a journal of their thoughts during the adoption process to give to the child at a later date. Other family members can include their memories and well wishes in the journal as well. The journal may also include a family history, information about relatives, and genealogy that might be of significance to the child at a later date. This not only allows the birth parents an outlet to express their feelings of love, but later provides an opportunity for the adopted child to comprehend the situation and realize they were not abandoned or unwanted.

In open adoptions, it is imperative to finalize the placement with a post-adoption contract agreement. This is an agreement between the adoptive parents and the birth parents regarding the expectations and nature of the relationship between the child and the birth parents. It clearly states the manner of contact and the frequency of visits. It may also clarify if and when the child is told of their adoption. Visitation expectations are clarified for other family members such as grandparents, not just the birth mother and/or birth father.

If there is not actual physical visitation but if updates are sent to the birth mother, the agreement states a schedule as to the frequency of the updates, pictures included, address changes, and other details. It can later be changed to fit the needs of either family, but it helps the transition by clearly stating expectations and behaviors from both parties. The more precise and specific the document, the less chance of disappointment and tension between the two sets of parents in the following years. The agreement also gives all parties a sense of security in knowing what to expect or allow, as well as what behaviors or events will not occur. So many times, fear of how one set of parents will react causes more turbulence than the actual communication and negotiation of the issue.

Birth Mother—Back to Normal Physically

During the entire pregnancy, a woman's body experiences drastic changes both externally in size and shape, but also internally with fluctuating hormones. These changes do not stop after the birth of the child, as now the body goes through physical stages to return to "normal." A physician will inform his patient of these stages and what to expect along the journey back to their pre-pregnancy body. In the case of a birth mother, some aspects of her life may take a different route, or she may not be in contact with a physician and need more support from friends and family.

In most adoption cases, the baby is only breast-fed a few times, if at all. This leaves the birth mother to dry up her breast milk shortly after the birth. Typically, it should take roughly seven to ten days for the breasts to stop producing milk. During the first few days, the breast will become extremely full and heavy, a condition called engorgement. The breasts are often tender and uncomfortable during this time. It is critical that the woman does nothing to increase the production of milk. If she expresses milk to relieve pressure, it stimulates the production of more milk and delays the process of drying up. It is also advised not to allow anything warm on the breasts, as this also stimulates milk production. Although it may sound tempting, a warm shower should be avoided as it can cause milk production to resume.

If the breasts are painful, cold compresses can aid in decreasing milk production and offering some relief for the woman. If milk production hasn't stopped in two weeks, then she should seek assistance from a health professional. (At one time, drugs were prescribed to aid in this process, but they were later found to be unsafe and are no longer on the market. However, a doctor can monitor the progress and offer suggestions to assist in the transition.)

Most women desire to lose the weight gained with pregnancy and to return to their pre-pregnancy size. Breast-feeding does aid in the loss of weight, but if the woman is not breast-feeding, there are still many options to lose the pounds gained in pregnancy. It is crucial to examine the situation as a long-term process to health, not just a quick fix to lose a few pounds. The women who are most successful are the ones who focus on a balanced nutritional plan combined with a schedule of regular exercise. Fad diets and quick solutions are usually unsuccessful. They may work temporarily; however, women typically regain the weight later just as quickly as they lost it. Pregnancy drains the body of various essential vitamins and minerals, and fad diets may intensify the problem resulting in poor overall health.

If the birth mother remains under a doctor's care, then it would be wise to ask for advice on a nutrition plan that will help in weight loss. Once a reasonable eating plan is established, it becomes important to find time to incorporate exercise on a daily basis. Not only does this aid in burning calories and losing fat, but it also stimulates the production of endorphins, which have been shown to improve mood and overall mental health. As the body changes physically, the hormones return to pre-pregnancy levels. This change in hormonal levels can cause intense mood swings, and while exercise will not cure or stop these, it can actually alleviate the drastic fluctuations. Exercise provides an outlet for relieving stress and emotions in a constructive way.

Some find it easier to adhere to a fitness plan if they have an exercise buddy. It could be another woman who recently went through childbirth, a friend, or family member. Incorporating another person usually makes exercise more fun while each of you can hold the other person accountable for their fitness and weight loss goals. As the woman witnesses her body returning to its natural form, it boosts self-image and esteem. Exercise drastically shortens the time span it takes for a woman to return to her normal body and greatly improves her mental health.

The uterus takes six to ten weeks to return to normal size, and doctors typically recommend waiting at least six weeks before engaging in sexual intercourse. Much of this advice is determined by the amount of swelling and soreness the woman experiences. Sexual desire may take even longer to return, simply because of hormonal fluctuation or possibly the fears associated with pregnancy. One common myth is that you cannot get pregnant if you are breast-feeding or right after childbirth. This is false, and many women get pregnant within weeks of giving birth.

The young woman's physician should establish a plan for birth control as a part of her follow-up exams after the birth of the child. If she has concerns about her sexual life, it is important to communicate these to the doctor to get an informed medical opinion, not just a myth without scientific basis or advice from a well-meaning friend who lacks the correct medical knowledge.

Back to Normal—Emotionally

Every mother who gives birth experiences mixed emotions as her body recovers and as her hormone levels attempt to revert to normal. This journey is often full of rough spots and uncertainty for the recovering woman. Birth mothers experience all the normal side effects of fluctuating hormones, but they also live with the turmoil of grief for giving up their child. The weeks immediately after the relinquishment of the child usually coincide with the birth mother's most intense grief for her child. This is normal and should be expected. Grief is a means of dealing with emotions when relationships are severely changed through circumstances such as divorce, death, theft, or other types of separation. Giving up a baby for adoption is a loss to the birth family.

There are actually two separate kinds of grief. The first type of grief is the actual loss the person experiences. If it is a loss of a relationship or a person, then the grief manifests itself as the yearning for this person to continue to be in one's life. In the case of the birth mother, it is the loss of a baby that she felt growing inside her for nine months. There is a bond that develops between the fetus and the mother during the pregnancy. When the baby is no longer connected to the mother and no longer with her, there is a great sense of loss that must be faced.

For other losses of relationships, such as death and divorce, there is a public acknowledgment of what the person is experiencing. Typically, there may be a funeral or other instance where friends and family offer public support and condolences for the loss. With the loss of an adopted child, many people may not even know the mother had a baby. The adoption may also be viewed with a sense of shame within a family, so no one ever mentions the event. The birth mother is often left to deal with her emotions of the loss entirely on her own even though she may have others around her.

It is also notable that many of the friends, associates, and family around the birth mother may treat the adoption as a relief. They are happy that the baby is with adoptive parents who will give love and opportunities for the child. While this is true, it doesn't lessen the fact that the birth mother must navigate through the grieving process of losing the child. She cannot be expected to simply "get over it." Every individual is different, and the time frame of the grieving process varies from person to person. It is critical, however, that the grief be acknowledged, or the mother may move into denial and bury her emotions. This may seem like a means of survival at the time, but the emotions will resurface later and can lead to destructive behaviors. The sooner they are dealt with, the sooner the healing process occurs.

A journal is an excellent tool to express the emotions and thoughts a mother experiences without fear of judgment from others. The birth mother must understand that the flood of her emotions are normal and that eventually she will gain control. It is a very uncertain time, and family should offer support and love for the feelings she is experiencing, not the feelings they "think" she should be feeling. There is no correct way to grieve, and there is no perfect time frame.

The other kind of grief is for future experiences that will be missed. As in a death or divorce, the person grieves missed opportunities, celebrations, and milestones that will not include the missed individual. With the example of the birth mother, she may grieve for future birthdays, the first day of school, or the first date that she will not be able to witness. She may grieve that she cannot truly be involved in the development of her child even if the adoption were open. She may question her identity. Was she really a mother? Can she be a good mother if she decides to have children later in life?

The mother's sadness from giving her child up for adoption never fully disappears. The grieving process simply allows the woman the ability to handle the sorrow and to integrate it into her life in a way that helps her move forward. Realizing that she will never fully eliminate the loss—nor should she—often assists the woman in moving on to acceptance. Navigating through the grieving process does not mean that she is "forgetting" her child, but simply accepting the loss and gaining some control over the situation and her emotions.

The mother may also grieve her loss of opportunities either in the educational or job setting due to the birth. She may have to quit school for a while or lose a job due to her pregnancy. Even if she is allowed to return to the same life she had previously, she may still feel a loss of time. Friends may be farther along now or gone. If she is not allowed to return to her previous life, she may experience an intense sense of regret and even a loss of identity. She may constantly ask, "What should I do now?" She may also become extremely critical of herself or may experience shame. Her inner voice may say, "I was so stupid. I deserved what I got. I don't deserve to be successful." All these negative thoughts are common but extremely detrimental for a young woman to feel toward herself. If she focuses on these statements, it becomes important to find an outside person to offer a voice of reason to counteract this destructive thinking pattern. The mind is powerful, and the thoughts she chooses to focus on will later manifest themselves in her life.

The mother may also grieve the loss of other relationships in her life during this time period. Often, her relationships with her parents, family, and even friends may disintegrate or drastically change because of the unexpected pregnancy or her decision to put the child up for adoption. She may undergo a feeling of loss of their acceptance and love, especially if her parents were unsupportive of the decision. There may also be issues with the father of the baby. Many times the pressures of the pregnancy cause the relationship between the birth mother and father to deteriorate, leaving the mother with a tremendous sense of abandonment to deal with alone. Again in this scenario, she is experiencing all the physical side effects of childbirth, as well as the emotional grieving of losing a child and a relationship with the birth father. She is, however, often expected to handle it all on her own—an especially difficult feat considering that many birth mothers are very young with little life experience. The entire process seems daunting.

It is critical for the mother to find support in some way that fits her situation. Some ideas for possible avenues to find help include the following:

- Adoption counselors—Many agencies offer ongoing assistance to their birth mothers.
- Mental health organizations—Most communities have mental health professionals to help with grief and depression issues.
- Support groups—Meeting with others experiencing the same emotions and thoughts offers a sense of acceptance and helps the healing process.
- Online blogs or chats—These can be another form of a support group. They provide another means of connecting with others dealing with the same issues if the mother lives in a rural setting and has no others close by in her situation.
- Family/friends—Individuals close to the mother who offer unconditional support and love, as opposed to judgment, greatly improve her progress in the grieving process.

Relationships

The act of giving birth to a child forever affects the mother and, as a result, affects the relationships she currently has or will eventually develop. A mother who keeps her child typically engages with other women with children at day care, the nursery at church, the park, and in other situations. People see her out in the community and view her as "a mother." However, when a young woman places a child up for adoption, she is still a mother although society does not readily view her as such. Her relationships are affected by the decision because it deeply affects her. She does not, however, outwardly appear to be a mother and retains the discretion to reveal that fact if she so chooses.

As the birth mother experiences a time of grief and fear, often her parents or grandparents experience a period of adjustment as well. They grieve the loss of a grandchild, and they sometimes question how to view their daughter. Should she be treated as a woman ready to make her own decisions, or is she still "their child"? Much depends on the age of the woman, the type of adoption chosen, and the amount of contact the grandparents have—all of which affect their relationship with their own daughter. Many birth mothers report that after the birth of their child and adoption, their parents are overprotective. They do not want the woman to make another "mistake," as it's often called, so they try to monitor her behavior and location at all times. Even if the birth father is still a part of the young woman's life, the grandparents are more skeptical of his intentions.

It is important to communicate at this point because the birth mother's parents are not totally unjustified with their concern. They want what is best for "their child," just as the birth mother wants the best for her baby. They do not wish for her to experience any more pain in her life than necessary. In contrast, the young woman cannot feel as if they are simply patrolling her behavior and waiting for her to "mess up," as this will neither improve their relationship nor aid in her healing from the experience.

The other issue often seen between the birth mother and her parents is a failure to mention the birth or the child as though it had never happened. It remains an unspeakable topic that no one discusses. Life resumes as if nothing ever occurred. This lack of acknowledgment is also an unhealthy behavior because both sides are repressing emotions that inevitably will damage the relationship. For the grieving and healing processes to occur for all involved, the lines of communication must be maintained. A young woman's relationship with her family is critical to her future relationships with other individuals, men especially. Open communication is essential; if a counselor is necessary, then the birth mother and her parents should readily agree to the process.

In years past, it was much more common for a young woman to live at a maternity home once she began showing and return home after the birth. To friends and family, she looked much as she did pre-pregnancy when she returned. Often when she returned home, very few people, if any, knew that she had given birth, much less placed the child up for adoption. These secrets weigh heavily on the birth mother's recovery process and her ability to move on with life.

In recent years, pregnant women have been accepted more readily, and very few leave to give birth in another location. The news of the pregnancy is not as big a secret. When you add the fact that open adoptions are more prevalent, it means more family members are involved with the birth child. The adoption is not viewed as the deep dark secret that everyone avoids mentioning around the woman or her family. Even though society continues to place judgment on the birth mother, it is typically not as harsh a judgment as in years past.

But what about future relationships? When does a young woman explain to a future significant other that she gave a child up for adoption? What exactly does she say? Even discussing the past with future platonic friends may prove difficult. Of course the initial conversation may prove awkward, and she may risk feeling judged. But living a life with this secret takes a tremendous toll on a person's level of happiness.

For a strong bond to grow within a relationship, honesty and communication are critical. It is up to the individual personality of the birth mother as to whom she tells and how many people she shares her experience with. She may again want to solicit the help of a close family member or friend. The important aspect is that she is honest and forthcoming with those individuals with whom she wants to pursue a close relationship. The adoption is a significant part of her being. In order for others to build a relationship with her and truly love her as a person, they must know the events that shaped her life.

In the case of open adoptions, it is a priority for the birth mother to develop a relationship with the adoptive parents. Taking great care to follow the boundaries of the adoption agreement, she should maintain the contact that is expected and keep her responsibilities. If she does not keep her visits as planned or produce information as needed, then her relationship with the adoptive parents and with the child can be severely damaged, later resulting in tension and, possibly, less contact. Keeping the communication lines open and available creates a climate that is less stressful for both sets of parents.

CHAPTER SUMMARY

- Relinquishment of the child cannot occur until after the birth.
- The birth mother will experience numerous emotions after placing her child up for adoption.
- The birth mother needs a support system provided by family, friends, or counselors.
- It is important for the birth mother to take time to grieve the loss of her child.
- Honesty is important for future relationships to develop in a healthy way.

QUESTIONS

1.

2.

3.

4.

5.

6.

7.

8.

9.

10.

CHAPTER *five*

The Decision to Contact

Prior to the 1970s, the typical adoption was a closed one. Neither birth parents nor adoptees questioned the laws or requested opening the sealed adoption records as it simply was "not done." Adopted children may have wondered about their birth parents, and certainly those same birth parents often wished and yearned to know the child. However, the legal avenues to open communication were not yet established to provide the opportunity for all parties to meet.

By the mid-1970s, a group of birth parents formed an organization to lobby for adoption reform. Concerned United Birth Mothers (CUB) offered support for women involved in the experience of adoption. They provided a voice for legislation to open adoption records and ultimately assist in the reunion of birth parents with children lost through adoption. Other organizations chose to fight these reforms and preferred the legal situation to remain the same as it had been for decades. CUB was often portrayed to have a radical agenda totally against adoption, and while individuals within the organization may have shared those views, it also provided networking opportunities for birth mothers to share, grieve, and recover. Later, CUB became instrumental in the education of birth parents who wanted to search for adopted children. Despite CUB's controversial nature, it initiated the legal reform for the open adoptions so prevalent today.

Most women who placed their children up for adoption prior to the 1970s never truly considered the possibility of searching for their child someday. They returned to the life they knew, tried to recover, and moved on often without anyone or few people who knew of their experience or ordeal. Reunions were not discussed, much less organized, or promoted. Closed adoptions were simple and final.

Over the next three decades, tremendous changes occurred to the judicial view of adoption. More and more birth parents and adoptees pushed for the records to be opened. Adoptees filed to gain free access to basic information about their births that 98 percent of the general population received and often took for granted. Discrimination lawsuits were filed, and some adoptees even won.

Currently, most adoptions are encouraged to be either open or semi-open to allow for some communication between the birth parents, adoptive parents, and child. Each adoption can be drawn with individual boundaries and agreements to meet the specific circumstances of the individuals involved. Reunions are common with many support groups and organizations to promote the reconnecting of adoptees with their birth parents.

The power of the Internet with open access to databases of public information and other search services also paved the way for reconnecting with someone lost through adoption. And it is not just the birth mothers doing the research. Adopted children seek out their birth parents just as frequently. Registries are maintained where anyone involved with a previous adoption can enter known information to see if they connect with a possible match. The entire adoption climate is different. It is much more accepted in society and by parents today; both birth and adoptive parents are not subjected to judgment and the scrutiny as in years past. However the adoption process has evolved, it still creates a stressful situation when a birth parent reconnects with or meets the adopted child for the first time. The process of gaining the information to assist the reunion may be easier, but the emotions of the situation remain the same as does the stress.

Getting Ready—Birth Parent

A flood of emotions should be expected once a birth parent decides to initiate contact and, possibly, meet their child. The decision should not be taken lightly because many individuals are affected, even if it is in a positive manner.

One of the first things a birth parent should consider before searching is their motivation for conducting the search. Is it curiosity? Is it to try to make amends for previous behavior? Is it to try to find a sense of love or connection? Once the individual answers these questions, it should be evident if they have healed emotionally from the actual adoption or not. They may not feel emotionally stable when they discuss adoption, which is an indication that they may not be ready to take this step. If the birth parent seeks out their adopted child, or if they are more concerned about their own well-being—and not that of the adoptee—then they should allow more time to prepare before the initial contact. Support groups or counseling can help with the process. The reunion will most likely stir up old emotions from the past as well as create a myriad of new ones. When the birth parent is emotionally unstable, then they bring additional issues into the adoptee's life, which is definitely not a desirable circumstance.

Birth parents must come to terms with their fear before meeting at a reunion. Many fear the child will be angry with them for the adoption, which may be true in some situations. But the anger can be dealt with once communication and contact are established. Some adopted children report years of anger toward an unknown birth parent. However, once they actually meet each other and the circumstances of the birth clarified, the anger often dissipates quickly. If, however, the birth parent allows the fear of this anger to paralyze his or her search for a reunion, then reconciliation never occurs. The birth parent continues to live in torment and fear while the adoptee lives in anger.

Another fear birth parents experience revolves around meeting the expectations of what the adopted child envisioned of his birth parents. The parent may not feel successful or wealthy enough; they may be ashamed of their looks. Self-esteem may be an issue. Many times birth mothers were treated with such judgment and shame that they often develop low self-esteem, which haunts them for the rest of their life. They feel as though, no matter what they accomplished in life, it would never be enough to make up for their "mistake." Later, if they seek a reunion with the adopted child, these feelings of unworthiness can take on a debilitating nature. While some adopted children may have dreamed of a rich or famous birth parent, they really simply want to reconnect or to know information and attributes about their birth parent.

The adopted child cannot be put in the position of feeling responsible for lifting or building the birth parent's self-esteem. The adoptee has his or her own emotional issues to deal with. It is important that the birth parent work to maintain a high sense of self-worth before reuniting with a lost child. Often, after the reunion, a sense of relief or forgiveness is felt by the birth parent, but this does not always happen. To ensure the reunion is as healthy and beneficial to all parties as possible, it is important to deal with other emotional issues along the journey and not bring them into the new relationship with the adoptee.

There are often other individuals to consider once a birth parent decides to search for the lost child. Most often there are new relationships in the birth parent's life who will be affected by the introduction of the adopted child into his or her world. If there are other children, how will they react to the news of this new brother or sister? What fears might they possess? If there is a spouse, how will they handle the revival of a past that doesn't include the significant other? Many questions are asked and need to be answered. Will these questions bring up past behaviors and choices that are difficult to justify or answer?

Family communication remains the most important key for a unified effort at a reunion. Children and spouses must feel reassured that they may ask questions and state their fears. They must feel an unconditional love as well because the news of a new sibling can bring doubt or anxiety about a potential usurper. They may even feel guilty. "If Mom gave up a child, then why did she choose to keep me?" Some searches take years to connect, but with advancements in technology, others are almost instantaneous. It is important that the birth parents share their desire to reconnect with an adopted child before they actually initiate the search to eliminate the possible shock factor when the reunion takes place. If everyone is given adequate time to adjust to the idea of a new relative, then the transition typically goes much more smoothly.

Birth parents often report that they were able to manage many of the emotions associated with the adoption until they started to search for the child. They repressed the emotions or detached themselves from the grief. They may have experienced sadness on the child's birthdays, but for the remainder of the year, they tended to continue on with life and never dealt with the hurt. However, once they initiated the search, then feelings of doubt, shame, guilt, and extreme sadness arose in their everyday lives. It is frightening when this occurs because they are dealing with emotions from many years past and may feel as if they are losing control. In reality, they are experiencing grief (as discussed in a previous chapter). Grief can happen immediately, or it may take many years to surface. The doubts resurface as a birth parent wonders if he or she made the right choice by giving the child up for adoption instead of keeping him or her. Shame is sometimes felt from the birth mother's family and society. A birth mother can again feel as if she is unworthy to be a parent.

While all of these emotions are legitimate and certainly understandable, they all pertain to choices made in the past. It becomes imperative for the person experiencing these emotions to refocus on their behavior and choices in the future because they can control these. Worry and guilt can change the past. Birth parents should focus their emotional energy and to build their self-esteem and provide positive opportunities for their future.

If the birth parent chooses to search for the adopted child, then the focus should be on creating a loving, positive relationship with that person, not focusing on the past and regret. If they still feel shame, then they should seek counseling or a support group. Sometimes, volunteering at a pregnancy center offers an outlet by supporting other young women facing the tough decisions of an unplanned pregnancy. Helping others remove the focus from themselves and their past regrets often allows a birth parent to refocus on positive things they can change and control.

Adoptee—Getting Ready

Birth parents and adopted children search for their birth families at about the same rate. Adoptees frequently search for their birth parents but often for different reasons from the parents' reasons. They usually are curious, or they may have medical issues that only the biological family medical history can clarify for them. They typically wonder about genealogy, family attributes, and the circumstances of their birth. Sometimes adoptees simply want to meet a relative who looks like them. Even still, adoptees experience an emotional journey just as birth parents do along the path toward reunion.

The most prevalent emotion most adoptive children feel as they search for their birth parents is fear of rejection. From the time they found out they were adopted, they may have thought they were unwanted, a mistake, or abandoned. If the adoption was closed, then they may question its circumstances. They may wonder if their birth mother was a victim of a crime (e.g., rape) or committed a crime (e.g., drugs). The adoptive parents play a key role in alleviating these fears and reassuring the adoptee about his or her worth and value. Yet, a search for a birth parent will reveal many unknowns: Will the birth parent want to be found? Will they accept the child back, or will the emergence of the past bring them pain? Are they even still alive?

Many feel that the rejection through the act of adoption is enough. If they endure further rejection, some adoptees may think it too great an emotional toll. Fear can cripple the adoptee and the birth parent, but it should not hinder a reunion if that is the goal for both parties. Fear of the unknown is often much stronger than reality.

Betrayal and guilt often overtake the adoptee who searches for his or her birth parent. The adoptee can feel as if he or she is forsaking or hurting the adoptive parents by looking for the birth parents. How the adoptive parents explain the adoption and their reaction to the search play a critical role in the adoptee's feelings as the adoptee tries to make contact. Sometimes the adoptive parents even feel threatened or betrayed.

Communication among all parties improves the situation and often decreases unrealistic fears. The adoptive parents may feel they will lose their child or that their relationship will be hurt by the reintroduction of the birth parent into their lives. In most instances, the new relationship simply allows the adoptee to feel a deeper sense of gratitude toward the adoptive parents.

When an adoptee decides to look for his or her birth parents, it is important for the adoptive parents to know of the search. Nothing causes more stress and hurt feelings than being caught off guard by the news that their adopted child is planning a reunion with their birth mother or father—even if that child is in their thirties or forties. Secrecy creates more fear for both the adoptee and the parents, so open lines of communication to express these fears builds trust and bonding rather than a deterioration in the relationship. If a child finds his or her birth parents and develops a loving relationship with them, it does not take away from the love the child feels for the adoptive parents. The adoptive parents should not feel guilt; they are still the parents, both legally and emotionally. A reunion with a birth parent does nothing to change that fact.

Sometimes adoptees are fearful of a reunion with the birth parent because they feel as if they may not meet the birth parent's expectations. They may not feel successful enough, athletic enough, or smart enough. These fears are very common and similar to what the birth parent may feel before he or she meets the adoptee. Again, this is a problem with self-esteem, and a support system of family and friends or counseling helps alleviate the pressures associated with this kind of fear. Even if a reunion is not sought by the adoptee, he or she may still have thoughts about worthiness in the eyes of the birth parent. In this case, the adoptee should seek help to explore those feelings as they are detrimental to a positive lifestyle and can result in negative behaviors and outcomes.

The decision to initiate a search for either a birth parent or adopted child should not be made hastily; many different people will be affected—positively and, possibly, negatively. It is an exciting time, but those searching need to have supporters to face the outcome, whether it be positive or negative. Someone undertaking a search should not do so alone.

CHAPTER SUMMARY

- The decision to search for a lost family member stirs many emotions.
- Fear of the unknown is the greatest obstacle facing those seeking a reunion.
- It is a good idea to join a support group or go to counseling if the person is struggling with issues about the adoption.
- A search may take a very long or very short period of time.
- All individuals, whether the one searching or the one searched for, will experience a range of emotions once the search has been completed.

QUESTIONS

1.

2.

3.

4.

5.

6.

7.

8.

9.

10.

CHAPTER *Six*

Contacting—Do All Roads Lead to the Same Destination?

April 1985

Janet,

I had a feeling that you couldn't keep your mouth shut when I talked to you on the phone. The information you want is not for sale anymore. You know who got the information plus a whole lot more. Tell all your friends thank you for helping you out. You saved yourself some money but lost your son again. This time for good.

No signature

The search for a child placed in a closed adoption can be a long, arduous journey full of misinformation and dead-end leads. The search may even bring you into contact with untrustworthy individuals. The Internet and other technologies make it easier to search databases and connect through adoption registries, but many state laws still prohibit the disclosure of data from a closed adoption. States' adoption laws vary, and some have previously opened files for a short time only to close them again after succumbing to pressure from an opposing organization.

The first step in the process of contacting a child from a closed adoption is becoming familiar with the adoption laws of the state where the proceedings were held. These laws change constantly, so there is the possibility that the laws have changed from the time of the adoption. Opening sealed adoption files is a controversial subject with strong proponents on both sides. Some believe that sealed records in a closed adoption protect all parties involved from later distress and emotional turmoil that may arise from a reunion. They feel that opening records is detrimental to the entire adoption process, and argue that young women would be more likely to abort a child rather than risk contact with their grown child. Other groups strongly opposed to the adoption process feel that it takes advantage of young women and that babies are unwillingly taken from the birth mothers. In general, different groups lobby for laws that satisfy their agenda, and lawmakers sway among groups.

Getting Started

A search for an unknown individual is essentially the same whether you are an adoptee or the birth parent. A notebook or journal is an important tool in the search to compile facts, dates, and other helpful information. Start with what you know about the birth; things such as location, adoption agency, state of adoption proceeding, doctors' names, and other details that can provide clues for later. An original or amended birth certificate can also be important. Once you compile all your information, you will be able to start your search more easily. It is advisable to keep your notebook or journal with you most of the time to capture information and thoughts more readily. You should not rely on memory or jot critical information on a scrap of paper. This information collection and recording can assist you greatly if you decide to hire someone to assist with your search at a later date—not to mention the money you will save by having your information well organized.

Search for adoption registries and register your information. In some cases, you may be able to establish contact very quickly if there is a match. A popular web registry is the International Soudex Reunion Registry, the largest database in the world. This registry does not charge a fee (although donations are encouraged) and uses information only to match potential children and parents. It does not have a staff to conduct searches for individuals. Another popular registry for searches is the Adoptee's Liberty Movement Association (ALMA). This group charges an initial registration fee of $50 to cover administrative costs. ALMA does not provide a staff for searches but does assist members through local chapters and search assistants. There are many online directories and registries designed to reunite birth families with adopted children. You should choose the ones that best fits your needs and circumstances.

Another avenue that can greatly enhance your search is to seek a local adoption search and support group. They are often listed in newspapers, church bulletins, and the yellow pages, as well as online. There are two major benefits to these groups. First, you will be able to learn from the mistakes of others. Members may be able to explain laws or obstacles that you may encounter in your search. They can often orient you on shortcuts or key information in working with the judicial system. Some will offer recommendations on agencies or people that can help, or they may warn against certain individuals with whom they have had a bad experience. This networking not only offers numerous avenues and ideas for searching, but it also serves as a great source of information for people who have taken the journey on which you are embarking.

Another positive aspect about participating in a support group is the emotional support it offers you. Even when friends and family may show concern, the bonds formed with individuals who have experienced the same life-changing event as you can offer comfort.

You may also want to consider enrolling in an online mailing list that aids in search and reunions. These provide information and networking with people across the country. Adoption-oriented online blogs and chat rooms can benefit your search greatly.

It is important to gain as much knowledge about adoption laws in your area, reunions, and search methods as possible. Numerous books and articles are available at the library, in magazines, and online. The information you retrieve will help even if you later choose to hire a professional to conduct your search. It gives you a greater sense of empowerment to be in control of the search and to have been involved with the process.

Searching Choices

After compiling information on your case, you will likely need to choose how you want to continue your search. In the best-case scenario, you will find a match when you register with the online registries, and then it's a simple process to pick up the phone or send an email. However, if you did not make contact or find enough information, then you must proceed in a different manner. There are several types of assistance available to aid you in your search.

In most states, an established confidential intermediary (CI) system is in place. The intermediary is trained in gathering confidential information on the adoption and relinquishment of a child in a discreet manner. The CI can be recommended or appointed by the judicial system or an adoption agency that has been petitioned by the searching individual. (A petition is an application from an adult who wishes to find a relative. It provides information on the person sought as well as the individual conducting the search and that person's motivation.) The CI works alongside the person obtaining the petition for information.

Anyone over eighteen can petition for a CI, including the birth mother, the birth father, siblings, grandparents, the adoptee, or the adoptive parents. If the person sought is found and the person petitioning for the search gives mutual consent to communicate, then contact may occur. Once the court or agency is notified of the agreement, then the meeting can be scheduled. If either party refuses to exchange information or any communication, then the information and records are resealed and the case is closed. Fees vary according to the location of the petition, and there are no guarantees of success in the search. (Also, there are no refunds if the person sought refuses to communicate.)

Independent Search Consultants

Another, albeit more expensive, alternative is hiring an independent search consultant (ISC). ISCs are certified and more knowledgeable than volunteers or others working for a lesser fee. However, their fees tend to be lower until the person is found. The more information you can provide in the beginning stages, the less time and the lower your bill will likely be. Some individuals provide the service of searching without certification. They may be competent, but in general, they are not as thorough or as efficient as an ISC with certifications.

Certified ISCs know the intricate details of adoption laws, public records, and shortcuts through bureaucratic red tape. Although the price may deter some, the money and time spent searching by oneself often comes close to the fee charged by ISCs. If you opt for a searcher without certifiable credentials, make sure to get several references. To cut overall costs, a person may try to gather as much information as he or she can and research the basic facts, later turning this information over to the ISC when more expertise is needed. This initial legwork can cut the time spent searching and, consequently, the fee by more than one-half for a full-length search.

Private Investigators/Online Searchers

Some individuals opt for hiring a private investigator (PI) to conduct their search. These may be expensive, but they also may not charge unless the search is successful. Most private investigators handle a variety of job assignments, so it may prove difficult to find one with expertise in adoption cases. As with the ISCs, it is good practice to find one who is certified and has several references. Online searchers provide much of the same services as a PI, but you may never have face-to-face communication. Information may merely be exchanged by mail, fax, or email. The most critical aspect in choosing either of these avenues is credibility. It is a good idea to research several options before hiring someone. Checking out several possibilities also gives you leverage when discussing price and could help you determine if someone is priced beyond the range of others. You should also ask about the following with respect to the services sought: the time frame for the search, who pays for travel expenses, guarantees of success, and other issues. Be sure to have a written agreement to specify costs, hours, time frame, and any other aspects agreed upon before having the ISC or PI begin the search.

Self-Searches

Many people choose to handle a search by themselves or include only close family members or friends. Some enjoy the control a self-search offers and ensures that you will be the one who makes the first contact. The actual process for finding the missing person sometimes offers comfort to the person searching, particularly if it is the birth parent. A birth parent frequently wants to prove how much a child meant by devoting his or her time to find the child and establish communication.

The search is a learning experience that leads some people to volunteer and help others search once they complete their own. If they are able to incorporate family, bonds and relationships can improve through working together in the process. The downside to conducting a search yourself would be the time involved, the emotional investment, and the overwhelming difficulty at times. Each and every setback is taken harder when you experience it yourself than when you simply receive information about the progress of your search. At the same time, the joy of finding the person can bring a much greater sense of accomplishment through a self-search. Success through this route depends on the individual, financial resources, emotional stability, and stamina to wade through the sea of information and governmental bureaucracy.

Beware!

The emotional implications of a reunion with a lost relative leave individuals vulnerable. Sadly, there are people who make a living from unlawful and unscrupulous practices where they take advantage of others during this time of vulnerability. These predators may target a birth mother, offer services for exorbitant fees, and then extort more through threats of losing or even destroying all the identifying information. For these reasons, it is imperative that you choose someone with impeccable references and certifications. You also should have an explicit written agreement for payment, expenses, time spent, and results expected. One can avoid many conflicts and disappointments with explicit details in the initial contract of agreement. Do not let emotions or a sense of urgency push you into an agreement or business relationship with anyone who does not check out or who makes you feel uncomfortable. Trust your instincts about the people you come in contact with as you travel the journey to find your lost child or birth parent.

CHAPTER SUMMARY

- The first step to a successful search is gathering all available information and keeping it in one place, such as a notebook.
- Some sources of information are online directories, search organizations, and support groups.
- Adoption laws vary from state to state with respect to the availability of information. These laws change frequently.
- There are many individuals who search for a fee. It is important to check all qualifications, credentials, and references before hiring one.
- Beware of scams that prey on individuals and their emotions without providing results.

QUESTIONS

1.

2.

3.

4.

5.

6.

7.

8.

9.

10.

CHAPTER *seven*

Pressing On—Facing Obstacles and Setbacks

Once the search is underway, the person conducting it may encounter something unexpectedly difficult—waiting. So much emotion and thought went into the choice to initiate the search that the waiting may become much more difficult than originally expected. During the early phases, you may spend time gathering information and networking, but after a while, the searcher may have to wait on another person such as the CI or for a possible match in one of the registries. Sometimes leads offer promise and raise hope only to become a dead end. Developing a plan before encountering the obstacles and setbacks along the way may help ease the searcher's frustration and may help the person keep control over his or her emotions. Proactive waiting means finding productive exercises and methods to maintain a positive outlook while the search is underway. Before covering the specific exercises to assist the searcher, there is a brief discussion on the power of the Universal Laws of Attraction and Vibration. Once you learn to utilize this power to your advantage, then you become empowered to achieve more success in all areas of your life.

Law of Vibration

One of the most fundamental laws of the universe is the Law of Vibration, which states that all matter and things remain in a perpetual state of motion. Your cells, thoughts, and environment consist of molecules that constantly move in a vibration pattern called a frequency. Your thoughts change frequencies depending on whether they are positive or negative, and in either instance their strength is extremely powerful. The one thing about the Law of Vibration is that it is continual, and it always remains the same. It neither stops nor ceases to exist simply because someone denies it or remains ignorant to its presence. It is a constant.

Objects that produce the same vibration naturally attract one another despite the differences in their molecular makeup. Consider the wineglass that vibrates when a specific note is played on a piano. Even though they are not of similar makeup, their vibrations coincide and the glass resonates. Resonance is the state achieved when two objects attract because their frequencies are identical. Resonance also occurs with your thoughts and the results they attract. If you constantly harbor negative thinking and worry about all the wrong of the world, then these results will be attracted to you. Likewise, positive thinking will increase your vibration and will manifest itself in positive results. It is an extremely simple concept with amazingly complex applications. Therefore, it is critical to understand and harness the power of these laws so that they work for you and your success and not against you. There are many exercises that can help you gain control of your thought processes and utilize your power to attract whatever goal you desire.

Visualization

One of the best ways to create the dreams you desire and attract the outcomes you seek is through the practice of meditation or visualization. You gain control of your thoughts and focus on the desires you want. Your mental energy creates these positive thoughts that resonate at a vibration that matches the vibration of what you desire. According to this universal law, these objects or experiences must be attracted to each other as they reach the same frequency, called resonance. However, it remains extremely critical to maintain this positive vibration over an extended period of time. In many instances, people act positively and remain full of enthusiasm as they begin their search. However, as they experience dead ends and suffer setbacks, the enthusiasm wanes and negative thoughts enter their thinking. This is a critical time in the whole process, and allowing negative vibrations to take over will inevitably alter the events of a positive resolution. Therefore, you must restore and maintain the positive frame of mind at all times, not just during the beginning period.

One way to maintain focus is to establish a set of specific goals and then revisit the goals frequently. In the case of searching for a lost person, one of the goals would be to find the person, and another might be to establish a positive, loving relationship with them. Goal setting not only assists in the initial contact, but also helps set the tone for the relationship as it grows. Writing the goals in a place where you reread them daily, if not more frequently, helps you to imprint them into your thought process. Some individuals like to create a vision board where they write their goals or draw pictures of the achievements they desire in their lives. The board is placed in a prominent location, so they must look at it on a daily basis, constantly imprinting the goals into their thoughts. The list can be used to analyze behavior and actions, and you may choose to reevaluate your actions on a daily basis by asking, "Does this behavior fit into my visions or goals?" If it is obvious that the behavior is not conducive to the goals, then it is time to stop the behavior or reevaluate your goals.

Be aware that when you encounter setbacks or other negative circumstances, it will be more difficult to maintain your positive outlook. This is why it is so important to be proactive with a plan before you travel the rough stages. When any negative noise enters your thoughts, it is imperative to find your goals and reaffirm them repeatedly. You can consciously choose your mind-set. You are not helpless to the winds of change, but it requires diligence and commitment.

There are several methods for practicing visualization and meditation. The first requirement is that you have a quiet place and play soft, relaxing music. The time should be uninterrupted and of sufficient length to reach full relaxation. You cannot clear your mind and reach a beneficial meditative state if you plan for only five minutes before dinner is ready or if the children are talking to you through the door of your bedroom. However difficult the task may be to find individual time alone, it is critical to your success and, ultimately, to the success of others in your life as well.

As you close your eyes to relax, practice slow deep breathing to allow your muscles to release as well as your mind. Start to imagine the colors of the rainbow one by one. As you progress through each color, think about the emotions evoked by that color. Slowly examine your feelings through each one. As you complete the entire spectrum, your body should be in a totally relaxed state. Now is the time to reaffirm your desires into the conscious mind. Visualize the goals as already having been achieved. Imagine your life after the success of your achievement. How do you see life in one week, one month, or one year following the attainment of each individual goal or dream? After you replay your goals and future successes through your mind for a while, allow a quiet time to soak up the silence. Many believe this to be a time when God speaks to you or your consciousness reveals your inner strength. A quiet time without internal noise can bring a feeling of relaxation as well as productivity at the same time. The quiet time at the end of your meditation session is just as important as the actual visualization and should not be hurried or foregone.

Another method for improving your positive vibrations is through the expression of gratitude. You can show gratitude toward family, friends, and others who surround you in your typical day of life. Even as you display gratitude toward strangers, it increases your positive frame of mind, thus attracting positive situations. Not only does gratitude benefit you, but it also improves the lives of those around you. The choice to focus your attention on the blessings in your life improves your overall outlook and will manifest itself in other positive experiences. An example of focusing on gratitude is choosing ten items for which to give your thanks every morning before getting out of bed. Others may choose to focus on these items before retiring to sleep, and others may jot them down in a journal throughout the day. The timing is not as critical as the actual practice, but consistency of gratitude brings amazing results.

The complement to the expression of gratitude is offering forgiveness to individuals who have wronged you in the past. The freedom of this release of anger and hurt greatly improves the positive vibrations in an individual. In the example of birth parents, there may be family members or friends who did not support you in the way you needed. You may harbor resentment to the agency, a friend, or someone who didn't help you during your time of need. It also may be that the person you need to forgive is yourself. Many birth mothers live their lives constantly angry with themselves, or with persistent regret and doubt. It is not an easy process but can be willfully chosen and accomplished. Most importantly, it is necessary. A lifetime spent in anger gives rise to bitterness, which eventually will permeate every part of a person's life. In contrast, the forgiveness of past transgressions allows personal growth and a greater emotional outlook.

A great exercise to reach forgiveness is to list anyone from the past who has committed a transgression against you. Forgiveness is a choice not based on the transgressor's merit but on the act of forgiveness itself. It is constantly choosing to forgive so that you may continue to grow and heal. Repeat to yourself that you forgive the person or persons. If you begin to feel negative feelings or anger toward another person, rather than rehashing all their faults, begin to say your forgiveness statement about them. Say it several times. It is a conscious process until after enough perseverance you actually begin to "feel" the forgiveness. If the individual who needs forgiveness is yourself, then you must state your forgiveness as well as some positive attributes every time you start to talking about yourself in a derogatory manner. Sometimes the most negative things said about a person are self-directed. To surpass your limitations and fully move to achievement and happiness, it is critical to gain control of any negative, self-defeating thoughts and behaviors.

Journaling is another excellent method to incorporate visualization, gratitude, and forgiveness. Some people start each day by writing a paragraph listing all the things for which they are thankful. They continue with goals for the day or, possibly, the week—or any other time frame, for that matter. At times throughout the journaling process, they may stop and meditate upon a particular thought or revelation. Others journal before retiring to bed to reflect upon the day and analyze their thoughts at that time. If they haven't achieved all they expected or have experienced a setback or failure, then they use this time to reframe the thoughts into something positive before they go to sleep. It is important that you focus on positive experiences as you go to sleep and as you awake each morning. Your subconscious continues to revisit your thoughts as you sleep, so you want this period to be conducive to a positive frame of mind.

Have you ever awakened from sleeping to be angry or exhausted from frustrating dreams? Or maybe you cannot even remember a dream, but you feel angry or upset. Many times these experiences are influenced by the thoughts you focused on prior to entering the sleep pattern. The ability to manipulate your thoughts toward more positive energy before drifting to sleep empowers a person to control how he or she awakens the next morning.

Just as exercising muscles feels difficult and sometimes painful, learning mental exercises to improve your frame of mind and enhance your success may feel awkward and painful as well. There may be instances where you perceive that you must not be doing the exercises correctly or that it's simply not working. In the beginning, the results may not be earth-shattering or lift you to where you feel a huge difference. Persistence is the key. The more you practice, the more you improve—which later attracts greater success. It is important to try different exercises several times to help you determine which best fits you and your circumstances. Some things that prove difficult initially develop into a necessity later in your journey.

Just as any relationship requires a time commitment, you deserve a time commitment to the improvement of your outlook and your successes. Many people just are content simply to exist. They don't think about goals or anything they desire to achieve. They are complacent with their status in life and don't see a need to dream. In essence, they have shut the dreaming part of their minds off and convince themselves that the status quo is a fine place to be. These very same people would derive benefits from wonderful goals and opportunities if they simply would allow themselves the freedom to visualize and dream. Once you commit to improving yourself, achieving goals, and reaching dreams, you also become a more positive force to those around you. It is important to take care of your basic needs first, and then you are more useful to those around you. You are important! Never underestimate the power of your presence and the impact you have on others and the world around you.

CHAPTER SUMMARY

- Sometimes a search takes a long period of time with many obstacles. It is important to keep a positive outlook during this time.
- The Laws of Vibration and Attraction are constantly at work and greatly affect your achievement of goals.
- Visualization is an excellent practice to reach your desires.
- The acts of forgiveness and gratitude allow your thoughts to be more positive.
- Journaling is an excellent activity that allows for goal setting, an emotional outlet, and positive reframing.

QUESTIONS

1.

2.

3.

4.

5.

6.

7.

8.

9.

10.

CHAPTER eight

Parent Fears

The emotional roller coaster introduced by contact between a birth parent and adopted child brings many feelings and fears to both the birth parents and the adoptive parents. Most reunions end positively, but even favorable outcomes produce a range of emotions. Sometimes the shock factor of the situation enhances fears and uncertainties as the contact may seemingly come from nowhere. Anticipating these feelings and realizing they are normal can aid in diffusing their impact.

Birth Parents

In about one-half of reunions, a birth parent is the individual searching for the adopted child. In these cases, surprise is not an issue, but other feelings and fears are much the same as when the child is the searcher. The most common worry shared by the birth parents is fear of judgment from the adopted child and adoptive parents. The birth parent may believe the child may be angry because he or she was placed in adoption or may even feel abandoned and unwanted. If the adopted child's sense of abandonment later manifests itself as a stumbling block in life, he or she may blame the birth parent for these problems.

The birth parent may fear judgment from the adoptive parents as well. The adoptive parents may possibly think that, since she readily gave the child up once, she doesn't ever deserve the chance to reestablish any kind of relationship with the child. This fear of the birth mother is caused by how the birth parent was treated during the adoption process. Typically, birth mothers experience some guilt and shame during the adoption process and afterward. However, if family and friends also conveyed feelings of shame or that the birth was a "mistake," then the birth parent may harbor even deeper sensitivities of unforgivable shame and guilt. Counseling during the adoption phase could help with these perceptions; but if the parent faced her emotions by herself, then these feelings will most likely reemerge later in life. Deep, hurtful emotions, such as shame and guilt, cannot simply be repressed forever. Inevitably, they resurface, especially in the presence and reconnection with an adopted child.

Sometimes after the initial contact with the child, the birth parent feels a huge sense of regret. She replays life's circumstances and wonders, "What if?" What if she had kept her child? Could she have made it work? What if she had not lost out on so many years of the child growing up? Of course, these questions are understandable, but continually living in regret does nothing to enhance the future or better the new relationship with the child. It is important to refocus thinking into something positive so that it can bring about experiences beneficial for the future. Negative thinking cannot change the past.

A birth parent with low self-esteem may deal with the feeling that he or she does not "deserve" a relationship with the adopted child. She may believe she would become a burden in the child's life or may cause grief and disappointment. In the eyes of birth mothers, there is nothing positive they can bring to the child's life. This thinking pattern may often be attributed to the treatment by others and society during the adoption process. Many birth mothers struggle with a feeling of low self-worth after an adoption. However, most adopted children are not searching for someone famous or of great stature; they simply want a few answers or a presence in their lives. The birth parent's fear can actually stifle the relationship with the adopted child unless she comes to deal with her own low self-esteem.

After the contact is made and communication established, some birth parents report a deep sadness. They may want to cease the relationship because it simply brings a deep sense of remorse. Regret fuels their emotions, but it does not enhance their outlook on the future to a more positive point of view. Ceasing the relationship because of this sadness is not fair to the adopted child. This sadness is something that must be dealt with and worked through. But it is possible, and the birth parent should not give up on the relationship as it can grow into something that stops the heartache.

All of these emotions are typical and should be expected when traveling the unknown journey of reconnecting with an adopted child. However, if the emotions are crippling or change the tone of the relationship, then counseling should be sought. When the birth parent continues to live with negative emotions and in fear, she limits future joys and relationships with others. Seek a professional through an adoption agency, medical group, or church organization to deal with these negative emotions; it's critical to get help. There is no need to continue to live life facing these emotions in solitude.

The sentiments felt by birth parents are not all negative in nature. Most birth parents describe a sense of tremendous joy at finally meeting their child. Seeing what the child looks like, his attributes, likes, dislikes, and health help satisfy the year of curiosity. Many birth parents describe relief at finally having a "face" to put with their feelings. They go through life wondering how the child is, if he does well in school, and if he is healthy, but they never have a face to put with these feelings.

In most instances, the birth parent wants to explain the circumstances behind the decision to place the child in adoption. She may want to ask for forgiveness or simply make amends for the previous decisions. It is not the birth parent's goal to take the place of the adoptive parent, but simply to regain a place in the child's life. It is important for the child to know that the birth parent cares for him and that he was not "abandoned." Once the relationship grows and the birth parent feels he or she has received forgiveness or proven his or her concern for the child who was given up, a burden is lifted from the birth parent's shoulders. Many experience a sudden freedom—they can finally leave the past in the past without further regret.

Adoptive Parents

The reemergence of a birth parent in a child's life can greatly affect the emotions of the adoptive parent. They are the ones who nurtured the child and provided love and necessities. They are the true parents to the child. Oprah Winfrey states, "Biology is the least of what makes someone a mother." But when a birth parent reenters the picture, sometimes the adoptive parents feel as if the parenting lines fade. Are they still the "real" parent? Will their child view them differently? The fear of a lessened relationship or, at worst, a lost relationship with the child causes the adoptive parent to worry about the future. They may feel that if there is ever a disagreement within the household (which is inevitable with children and teens), the child will simply gravitate toward the biological parents.

Fear of the future and possible loss is common, but establishing clear lines of communication and boundaries within the new relationship will alleviate some of these emotions. When adoptive parents initiate and choose to build a relationship with the birth parents, it allows them to feel some sense of control of the unknown fears they face. Otherwise, most communication will probably occur between the child and the birth parents, leaving the adoptive parents feeling left out. It is much better for all involved when the adoptive parent is proactive to opening the lines of communication and building trust between the two sets of parents; it creates a sense of unity. Fear breeds resentment that creates tension and unhealthy relationships. Communication builds trust and offers a sense of security.

Sometimes the adoptive parents will feel a great sense of betrayal. This feeling stems from several different sources. They may feel that the judicial system betrayed them if their adoption was closed. In this instance, adoption laws and regulations wind up being "broken" or altered in later years later. The sense of security that adoptive parents believed they had through a closed adoption ultimately proves to be false, and now they must face many unknown factors. What are the birth parents like? Will they be dependable? Will they bring joy or hurt to the child's life? Will they try to come between the child and the adoptive parents?

In fact, the adoptive parents may feel the birth parents betrayed them by trying to resume contact with the child if they are the ones initiating the search. The birth parent agreed to a closed adoption in the first place. The adoptive parent may even question the motivation of the birth parents. Are they truly trying to do what is best for their child, or is their search for selfish reasons? Certainly, all of these are legitimate concerns and should be answered. The adoptive parents are the true parents and protector of their children. They have the right to know the background and motivation for any adult who has contact with their child. If the adopted child is older, then the parent has less say in his or her choices; however, the adoptive parent should still feel a part of the reunion. Alienating the adoptive parent will only create tension and cause heartache.

Finally, the adoptive parents may feel betrayed by their child. They may wonder why they are not "enough" as a parent. Why must they keep searching for someone else? Was I not a good enough parent, they may ask. Did I not do enough for them? This frame of thinking generally does not reflect the adopted child's rationale for making contact because very few adopted children search for their birth parents out of dissatisfaction with their adoptive parents. In fact, when the adoptive parents give their blessing to the search, it creates a stronger bond of trust between them and their child. A sense of insecurity during the reunion process should be expected, but should not override good judgment, and should not prevent communication among the adoptive parents, birth parents, and the child.

The adoptive parent can also experience positive emotions from a reunion when their child is happy. The adopted child may have asked questions about their birth, their birth parents, and other details that the adoptive parent could not answer. Witnessing the joy their child expresses from meeting their blood relatives, and having their questions answered often brings joy to the adoptive parents as well. Everyone yearns for his children to be happy and feel love. When this happens—even if the manner in which it occurs is unconventional—it still brings satisfaction to the child and the adoptive parent. The simple smile of a child warms the heart of any parent.

We are reminded of the biblical story of the prodigal son, although as it relates to this instance the roles are reversed. In the biblical story, a wealthy man has two sons. He gives both the sons their inheritance early in their lives. One of the sons stays with him, helps him, spends his money wisely, and is genuinely a great man. The other son is foolish and travels abroad, spends all his money in dishonorable ways, and basically winds up destitute. The father always wonders about the lost son and constantly awaits his return. One day he sees the son on the horizon walking home, and he runs out to meet him. He is so excited that he orders a fatted calf to be cooked for a large homecoming gathering. The faithful and wise son feels slighted. Who wouldn't? His father never threw him a party in all the years of being the faithful son. But the lesson is that just as a shepherd will look for the one lost sheep when he has ninety-nine in the pen, our Lord searches for us when we are lost.

An adoptive parent could feel slighted when the birth parent returns to the child's life. Why would my child look for the person who placed him up for adoption when I've been here all along, the adoptive parent might ask. Why get so excited about someone who really wasn't that involved in the child's life? Basically, they wonder, "What about me?"

Just because the child searches for the birth parent does not mean they have gripes or concerns about the adoptive parent. It has nothing to do with the adoptive parent's ability to parent successfully. The adopted child simply may feel that he or she needs to search for something lost in his or her life. The adoptive parent provided safety, security, and love, but the searching process does nothing to change that fact. Families are important, and reunions can be a critical turning point in all the parties' lives. Even though everyone is not exactly perfect, the relationships formed are critical to growth and understanding.

CHAPTER SUMMARY

- Both adoptive parents and birth parents experience many emotions and fears prior to a face-to-face reunion.
- Fear of the unknown is often felt by both sets of parents.
- Communication is critical to alleviating fears and building trust.
- If an individual carries negative emotions from the adoption itself, then it is important to seek help to work through these feelings before the reunion.
- Reunions can work and bring joy to all parties involved with the adoption.

QUESTIONS

1.

2.

3.

4.

5.

6.

7.

8.

9.

10.

CHAPTER *nine*

Adoptee Concerns

The circumstances surrounding an adoption play considerable roles in the development of the adopted child. These circumstances color their overall opinion of what adoption is and what it actually means. Children who grow up knowing they are adopted never truly experience a "shock" or emotional upheaval of discovering their adoptive parents are not their biological parents. The adoptive parents' attitudes and demeanor about the adoption impact their child's outlook in either a positive or negative manner. Many of these children possess a great feeling that they were "picked" or wanted so desperately that their parents went to great lengths and expense to find them. Other children may feel that they were "unwanted" and abandoned, and develop an issue with security and trust.

While their view of adoption and their value vary greatly by individual, most adoptees experience a curiosity about their heritage. Many times they choose to hide this wonder from the adoptive parents or even friends and family. But secretly they desire to know "where they came from."

What did my mother and father look like? What's my heritage? Why was I given up for adoption? They yearn to know if they look like someone from their biological side. In the world of today's open adoptions, many of these questions are answered as the child grows up. They are raised knowing their biological parents; and questions are answered as the child matures and wants to learn more, which helps prevent a sense of a void or an identity crisis.

Anger is another common emotion that adoptees may experience and need to work through. In some cases, they may not even realize they are truly angry inside. Later, they could feel guilty for harboring anger toward their biological parents. The emotion is common, but the act of harboring and allowing it to fester into bitterness is detrimental to one's emotional health. Many times they sense they were not loved, not worthy of love, and simply "thrown away." Again, circumstances of the adoption greatly affect these thoughts of self-worth. Were they adopted immediately to a loving family, or did they move from one foster family to another—or through several families? How were they treated subsequently? Were they always an integral part of the adoptive family, or were they sometimes singled out or allowed to feel "different?" These questions paint a vivid portrayal of how issues of trust and self-esteem develop and frustrate the adoptee later in life. Even children adopted into loving, well-adjusted families may face a sense of anger from time to time. Alternatively, they may feel that their adoptive family provides all the love they need, and they have no desire to contact the individuals who them up.

When an adopted child decides to search for his or her birth parents, it is common for the child to worry about the feelings of the adoptive parents. They may want to answer their curiosity, but they don't want to hurt their adoptive parents, either. Communication is extremely important during these stages because most adoptive parents are supportive and want their child to be happy. The adoptee may often feel as if he or she is betraying one parent for another or that his or her loyalty to the adopted family is somehow compromised by initiating a search. Even when the child is not the one conducting a search—but perhaps is found by the biological parents—he or she may still worry about how the adoptive parents' reactions.

The decision to search is a major one and shouldn't be entered without much consideration. Counseling or support groups are a credible option to work through emotions and to determine thoughts that may be a hindrance to personal development. Once an initial contact is made and a meeting expected, belonging to a support group can really aid in the journey to the initial face-to-face meeting. Adoptive parents also should be encouraged to attend some sort of support as well. In some instances, families attend together, but families may also attend as separate parties. The critical point is to realize that support is available once an individual chooses to search or to meet with the biological parent.

The time period between contact and the face-to-face meeting is exciting but can overwhelm individuals as well. Fear of the unknown causes distress and worry. The adoptee is often left wondering. He may ask some of the following questions:

- Will they like me?
- Will I be a disappointment?
- What if I don't like them?
- What do I call them?
- I don't even know them. How do I act?
- Will they expect me to hug them or show affection?

Finding a close person whom to discuss these fears and, at the very least, acknowledge their existence often alleviates some pressure. A meeting is a huge life-altering event; some anxiety is normal and should be expected. It is also important to realize that the biological parents are also experiencing many of the same emotions and worries as the adoptee.

The Meeting

Once the face-to-face meeting is agreed upon, plans should be made as to the duration and location of the visit. While some adoptees claim to feel anxiety as well as joyful expectations, others say they often feel numb about the whole experience until it actually happens. This confusion or lack of emotion stems from the uncertainty as to how this new person will fit into the adoptee's life. Where will the adoptee fit in the parents' lives? What exactly are they supposed to feel? It's not like looking forward to a visit from a favorite relative because there has been no previous experience or bonding between the two. Communication by email, mail, or phone builds the connection and allows bonding to start. Exchanging photos and family information can also ease some anxiety so that both individuals know a little more about what to expect.

It's a great idea to bring childhood scrapbooks, pictures, or other memorabilia to the reunion with the birth parent. It not only provides an opportunity for conversation, but it offers a small way to include the parent in the experiences of the adoptee's life—it paints a clearer picture of "who" their child really is. Another suggestion is to jot questions about one's heritage, the adoption, famous family members, and so forth. These can help stimulate conversation as well. Save some of the more difficult questions for later in the visit after some trust and security have been established. The adoptee should avoid confrontational or judgmental questions, and prepare for honest answers that may not fit exactly to his or her frame of thinking. Honest communication is the most critical component of a successful reunion and, possibly, a healthy relationship later on.

The adoptee also needs to prepare to offer forgiveness if the birth parent asks for it. It is very common for the birth parent to regret her decision and need forgiveness to move on in life. The act of forgiveness releases a person from negative emotions and allows healing to begin. Even if the adoptee doesn't realize he needs healing, forgiveness and acceptance of the birth parent bring a positive spirit to thinking about his adoption.

The adoptee should also be prepared to accept that the birth parent may have a different value system with respect to appearance and beliefs. Even though there may be many differences, it does not necessarily mean that the child and birth parent can't develop a supportive and healthy relationship. Many families have diverse views and interests, but they still maintain respect and fondness for all the members. It is important of the adoptee not to harbor expectations of the "perfect" parents or relationship because no two relationships are the same. It is healthier to realize that there will be differences but to commit to the development of the relationship anyway. The reunion may feel awkward initially, but honest, respectful communication will provide an opportunity for bonding and a more natural relationship to grow. Trust takes time and commitment to build. As the trust grows stronger, the relationship evolves into something more comfortable and significant for both parties.

Post-Reunion

In most instances, there is an emotional letdown after the face-to-face meeting. Several factors can contribute to this feeling, but the most common is simply the release of anxiety and stress. Expectations and fears about the meeting can keep an individual in a constant state of excitement, but afterward life returns to normal. This transition back to normalcy may even seem like a crash, and the person simply feels exhausted and emotionally drained. It should definitely be expected, and it is important to allow time to recover.

Continuing communication is important to foster the new relationship. Many birth parents give the adopted child space and let him or her dictate the pace and direction of the relationship. In fact, it may seem like work to make the effort to communicate with each other. Each call or email lays a foundation for a relationship. Distance between each other plays a significant role in the time it takes to build a relationship and the number of visits possible. It must be a journey taken together, and it requires the commitment of both birth parent and adopted child. One individual cannot make all the attempts at communication, and the other remain nonresponsive. A healthy relationship requires involvement by both parties.

CHAPTER SUMMARY

- Adoptees often must deal with anger and a sense of betrayal toward their birth parent.
- Fear is a common factor that adoptees feel when they are planning a reunion with their birth parent.
- It is important to approach the reunion with an open mind and without too many expectations.
- Adoptees often worry about how their adoptive parents will feel about the search.
- Communication is extremely important after the reunion to build a long-lasting relationship.

QUESTIONS

1.

2.

3.

4.

5.

6.

7.

8.

9.

10.

CHAPTER *ten*

Finally, the Meeting

There is no set protocol for arranging the face-to-face meeting of an adoptive child with his or her birth parents. Agencies and intermediaries offer advice and support, but ultimately it depends on each individual's needs and circumstances. These circumstances include finances, age of the child, location of the individuals, adoptive parents' wishes, and time. In addition, the emotional readiness of the adoptive child and the birth parents must be considered a primary concern; a personal meeting should not be scheduled until all involved feel prepared.

Communication and compromise allow for a healthier relationship, which precedes a more positive reunion. It is important that everyone involved feels comfortable enough to make his or her wishes known and that each works to reach a satisfactory agreement.

Time Spent Before the Meeting

The initial contact generally occurs by mail, email, or phone without a face-to-face meeting. After communication starts between the birth parent and adopted child, there is a period of time in which both parties feel a temporary shock or disbelief. Even the person searching may feel surprised and ask, "Did I really finally find them?"

Of course the person found may be caught off guard, and perhaps some time should pass before a face-to-face meeting is scheduled. Conversing through email and mail is easier and less threatening than a physical meeting. It allows both individuals to analyze their feelings without letting emotions dictate their responses. The next step would be phone calls, but these still offer a sense of emotional safety. The face-to-face meeting should not be planned until both parties feel prepared and not under pressure. Time should not be a factor as no two individuals react in exactly the same way. The most critical aspect of a successful reunion is that everyone affected be mentally prepared for the event.

Another reason to permit some time to pass before the meeting is that, in most cases, there are families and friends who need to be informed about the other person being found. In some instances, the birth parent may have hidden the adoption from the people in her life. A birth parent may need to explain to spouses, children, and friends about the existence of a previous child. This may seem like a daunting task, and adequate time should be allotted so that significant others are given enough time to process the new information. Even if everyone in the immediate family previously knew of the existence of the searcher, there should still bc a time frame to announce their reemergence into the other family's life.

The length of time between initial contact and a physical meeting is also dictated by the communication between the two parties. If they correspond daily via email, then the time may be shorter given a greater frequency of contact. If the contact is made by mail, it may take longer for everyone to become comfortable with the meeting. Again, the waiting time for the first visit depends on the individuals involved and how long it takes for them to achieve peace with the situation. If one struggles with the idea of meeting or communicating, then counseling is a great option to work through various issues and increase the likelihood of acceptance, growth, and peace in the process. It is also beneficial to all involved to consider a support group, either in person or online, to assist in dealing with the flood of emotions a reunion brings.

Who's There?

Another reunion concern involves determining which family members should attend besides the parents. This determination is also directed by individual adoption circumstances; however, whenever possible, the adoptive parents should also be included. (One must include the adoptive parents if the child is a minor, but even with children over the age of eighteen, many relationship difficulties are alleviated when the adoptive parents feel a part of the reunion process. It also provides the adoptee with the freedom of gaining support from both parents without feeling trapped in the middle or as if he or she is betraying one for the other.) It is beneficial when both parents strive to establish and maintain a consistent line of communication. This also prevents surprises such as a parent showing up without the other parents' knowledge. The ability to prepare and communicate concerns openly goes a long way in creating a positive atmosphere for the meeting. Ultimately, the emotional well-being of the child should serve as the motivating factor for communication and compromise between both sets of parents.

The main concern with involving other family members in the process is the comfort level of the adoptee and the birth parents. It can feel overwhelming for some people to meet a large group of people all at once while others may enjoy the attention and want to know anyone connected to their situation. An adopted child meeting with his or her birth parents may feel intimidated if he or she also meets half-siblings, aunts, uncles, grandparents, and friends all in one sitting. The birth parents should be considerate of this fact and, possibly, provide other opportunities later for a meeting with the extended family. If a considerable number of people are planned, it is a great idea to make notes on all the people invited and send it to the person to be introduced. These notes would provide basic knowledge on each person and their connection or relation, thus relieving some of the stress at the face-to-face meeting.

Location, Location, Location

The location of the reunion varies tremendously as well. The distance between the families and the duration of the meeting are determining factors in the visit. In all instances, it is less stressful on all individuals if the initial meeting place is at a neutral site or at least not at one person's home. This place could be a restaurant, a park, or even a vacation home. It may be easy to accomplish if both parties live reasonably close to each other, but what about instances where the traveling party has flown cross-country or even overseas? How is it possible to meet in a neutral zone then?

In many of these instances, the traveling individual is invited to visit and stay at the home of the other party. It is a great display of hospitality and also helps both parties to bond and get to know each other. However, the transition can be made a little more smooth if the first meeting is at a restaurant (possibly at the airport) or a short visit at a park or other area of local interest. This way, the visitor does not feel as overwhelmed by the surroundings at the initial face-to-face meeting.

The length of the initial visit is also dictated by the age of the adopted child. For minors, the visit should be shorter. With a child, more visits of shorter duration is more desirable than a visit for an extended period of time. Both sets of parents and the adopted child will experience an array of emotions during and after the meeting, so a lengthy visit may be extremely draining. If the reunion is a visit that lasts several days, then it is a good idea to vary activities and the time spent together. There should be some quiet times allotted for talking, asking questions, and getting to know each other. Depending on the hobbies and interests of the individuals, some other ideas for quality time include the following:

- Visiting extended family and friends
- Personal points of interest, such as schools attended or previous homes
- Sporting events
- A vacation home
- A day spa
- Local areas of interest—state park, amusement park, art museum, antique shopping

One of the problems with using the word "reunion" is that it is somewhat misleading. By definition, it is a reconnection between the birth parents and child, but in reality it seems much more like an introduction. There really are no shared experiences to relive. It is more accurate to describe it as a time of getting to know one another and the other person's likes, dislikes, interests, life stories, and so on. In fact, it could be called a "catch up" event since both parties try to condense several years of experiences into a short time span. Prior to meeting, it is a good idea for each person to write some questions he or she may want to have answers to and which may stimulate the conversation. Having the questions in advance in written form eliminates the problem of forgetting the questions at the meeting. Pictures from all stages of life, genealogy, and family heirlooms are also items that you may want to bring. Many adoptive children miss learning about their ancestors with different quirks or abilities. Often while sharing these stories, similarities between the birth parent and the child emerge, whether it is a favorite kind of pie, a fear of heights, or a school subject in which they excelled. All of these found similarities begin to forge a bond and create a sense of belonging. Common traits and interests serve as the foundation for a lasting relationship.

Much of the stress leading up to the first face-to-face meeting is founded in fear of the unknown. The following questions may arise.

- What if they don't like me?
- What if I'm not what they expected?
- What if we don't hit it off?

These are legitimate questions and concerns. In fact, at the end of the reunion, each person may realize that they are not too compatible and base their continuing relationship on those feelings. In those instances, at least the questions about the birth and subsequent adoption are answered, along with questions of heritage and medical history. The sense of "knowing" each other alleviates much of the stress and wonderment of just longing to answer questions. Hopefully, a relationship may still be possible and built upon through similarities and common interests. If both parties can meet more than once, then the stress and emotional upheaval should begin to dissipate with each additional encounter.

CHAPTER SUMMARY

- It's a good idea to allow some time for both parties to adjust after the initial contact but before a face-to-face reunion.
- Both parties should feel comfortable with the location, duration, and activities of the reunion.
- If the reunion is over several days, it is important to vary activities but to allow plenty of time to talk.
- When large groups of people want to meet the "lost" family member, it is a good idea to spread these encounters over several days.
- Every family has different interests and hobbies. It is nice to find activities of common interest.

QUESTIONS

1.

2.

3.

4.

5.

6.

7.

8.

9.

10.

CHAPTER eleven

And Now the Rest of the Story: How to Build a Relationship after the Reunion

The search and reunion process takes an incredible toll on the adoptee, the birth parents, and adoptive parents. After the person-to-person reunion, there is almost always an emotional letdown. Anticipation of the event keeps feelings stimulated prior to the reunion, but this passionate state cannot be maintained indefinitely. After the festive air clears and both parties return to their regular lives, they are left to sort through and analyze their feelings. This is not considered a negative experience but is simply a sign of growth. There are several stages that individuals associated with an adoption reunion will progress through. They may not enter all phases, and they may not progress in a given order. One should understand that these stages are quite normal in establishing and maintaining a truly healthy relationship, and this understanding can ease the transition through the process.

Honeymoon Stage

Once initial contact is made but prior to the face-to-face encounter, many individuals enter a euphoric state. In some instances, the simple fact of learning someone cared about them so much to spend time, money, and effort in a search allows the individual to feel wanted and loved. After the reunion, a time of simple joy and euphoria may continue. Both individuals may feel such a sense of belonging and enjoy finding out about their similarities. There is usually little conflict during this stage because the parties are typically focusing on learning more about the other person. The only discussion may be how to address each other, by either first names or by Mom, Dad, etc. They tend to be intrigued with one another, much the way a love relationship blossoms between two people who get married. They are concerned with the other person's happiness and often exchange small gifts and cards to express their feelings and show their love. This extreme happy period is usually temporary. Reality then sets in, and old issues may resurface in the relationship, causing the next stage to develop.

The Rest Area

Once the relationship progresses, affections grow stronger, and each party begins to feel that he or she is a more significant part of the other person's life. It may feel as if the relationship is advancing well at one moment while, in the next moment, fear of the significance becomes overwhelming. It is often during this time that fears set in because each individual may start to feel vulnerable. Since the adoptee may have felt abandoned at adoption, he or she may fear rejection again. As the adoptee's fondness toward the birth parent grows, he may realize or foresee the potential emotional hurt and anxiety if the relationship ends. It is most common for the adoptee to pull back or seem distant, but the birth parent may also have times of reservation. Individuals in the reunion process may need a brief time to pause and reflect on their emotions. It doesn't mean they are ending the relationship or that there are really any true problems. It just simply means that some time needs to pass before moving forward.

Individuals have different ways of handling this period. One may appear distant while the other still feels the need for closeness. The birth parent should not reject her child even if the child feels a need to pull back. Effective communication is imperative, but the fears of rejection of the adoptee are very strong and extremely difficult to overcome. If they are heightened by a growing distance from the birth parent, then a healthy relationship may become impossible. If the adoptee is the one pulling away, then the birth parent should offer space and unconditional support until the adoptee feels comfortable again. The birth parent should still maintain a presence through cards or an occasional email, no matter how far in distance. This allows the adoptee to maintain control of the significance of the relationship, and it empowers him to grow at his own pace. Since the adoptee had no control over the adoption or placement in the first place, the power of directing the relationship and how it proceeds provides a sense of safety and security for the adoptee. Once the adoptee is secure in his or her feelings and status in the relationship, then the adoptee feels comfortable in allowing it to evolve into something more significant.

Boundaries

There comes a time in any healthy relationship where each individual establishes boundaries or expectations about what he or she feels, wants, or needs from a relationship. This phase often overlaps with the previous phase as the boundaries are determined when each person reflects on his emotions. It is a time to determine how much contact is expected and what significance each will play in the other's life. Will they only correspond periodically and visit on major holidays, or will they be included in the everyday life and talk on the phone daily? Most often, the answer is found somewhere in the middle of these extremes, but it is dictated by the comfort level of all. Open communication and honesty play a considerable role in the development of the relationship past this point. If an individual only wants minimal contact, then the other party needs to respect that desire and avoid using guilt trips or emotional manipulation to try to make the person want more contact. There must to be a freedom to state one's feelings and know that they will be received without retribution. The entire adoption process is too complicated and emotional to continue with negative feelings during the reunion process. The only way to alleviate these thoughts is through honest and open communication. Otherwise, the feelings simmer and stunt the development of the future relationship.

An adoptee may pull away or set specific boundaries as a subconscious test of worthiness. He may not realize that he is doing this, but he does want to see if the birth parent is really willing to continue the relationship despite the difficulty. Adoptees pull back to see if the birth parent will keep a presence even when affection is not reciprocated. This pulling away is a common tactic that children or teens use with their parents in everyday life. They need to know they are valued in the relationship, not because of what they do but simply because of who they are. It makes sense then that this behavior carries over in an adoptee/birth parent relationship even when the adoptee may be an adult. This is a new relationship, and the adoptee's insecurity stems from being given up as a child. Adoptees want to test the strength or the sincerity of the birth parent before they proceed further in the relationship.

This need for reassurance will be decided by the role the adoptive parents played in the development of the child. If the child lived in an accepting environment of unconditional love, then they are less likely to experience as much insecurity. Children raised in awareness of their situation as an adopted child and offered a loving home from their adoptive parents usually grow into well-adjusted adults. However, if the child was not in an environment with loving adoptive parents, then security and fear may play a major role in the development of a relationship with the birth parent. These individuals should seek counseling in learning to deal with trust and insecurity because it was lacking during their formative years. Without such help, it will remain an obstacle until it is addressed. The birth parent of these children must provide a continual, consistent show of support and love so as not to strengthen the trust barrier. It may be a long journey, but the adoptee deserves a person to provide constant stability and support.

Once the adoptee and the birth parent analyze their feelings and expectations, then it is important to share them with the other party. It can be difficult to state feelings, particularly if they ask for less involvement from someone who wants to play a more significant role. Even though it may feel painful at the time or as if one person is hurting the other, the end result of this honesty is that the relationship can develop to a level and pace beneficial to both parties. Sometimes, a reunion may not go well. Perhaps the two parties share nothing in common or even clash over values, morals, or overall belief systems. Some may consider a reunion such as this to be a failure or a tragedy—when things don't necessarily work out as planned. However, even if the reunion does not turn out favorably, questions should still be answered. If the relationship does not blossom into something permanent or results in only a onetime meeting, it is important for the individuals to focus on the positive, not the negative. Look to the lesson learned, the knowledge gained; then move on from the situation. In these instances, the individuals may simply choose not to continue the relationship or choose to maintain very little communication, with the exception of medical emergencies or history. After that, both individuals should accept this outcome and continue with life—but with the gratitude that they did indeed experience a reunion and no longer have to wonder about the other person.

Solidifying the Foundation

The final phase of an adoptee and birth parent's relationship strengthening the foundation and moving toward the direction establishe during the boundary phase. Respect of the boundaries and expectations imperative to building a solid relationship. If, for instance, it was decid that contact should no longer continue by one of the parties, then